Fadi Gaziri

ZE GERMANS

also available as an ebook

Published by: epubli – ein Service der Neopubli
GmbH, Berlin

to my wife Stephanie

Contents

CH 03: German Language and Culture — 105

CH 04: Food & Leisure — 137

What are your
ROMANTIC
&
SEXUAL
intentions?

Foreword

I have been thinking long and hard about writing this book for a while now, but never had the courage to do so. This is mainly due to a scar I've been bearing for fifteen years - ever since university. I was in my final year at Durham, studying Music and German, and I thought it would be a great idea to take an interpreting course for one of my compulsory modules. It was a tough module, but somehow I managed to wing it through the first months without working too hard. I was good at speaking German, having spent a year there during my third year at university. My third-year professor, Mrs. Schumacher (a native German herself) loved the quiet, studious female students, the type that would always produce the perfect answer, written neatly on a piece of paper, but were generally very shy when speaking in front of the class. Basically, your typical *teacher's pets*. I fitted into that category like one of the Klitchko brothers in a Royal Ballet performance of *Swan Lake*. So it was quite natural that, from the very first lesson, she absolutely hated me. Months later, after a simultaneous translation test that had gone particularly badly — probably because I was still a student and preferred drinking in bars to studying in my tiny room — I remember Mrs. Schumacher handing me back a marked paper. As she did so, she looked at me with an overdose of *Schadenfreude* — one of the few German words that has made it into international vocabulary, roughly translatable as 'rejoicing in someone else's misery' — and said patronisingly, and I quote: "Considering that English is not your first language, you did pretty well, Fadi."

I was fuming, but managed to maintain the appearance of zen-ness, repeating the mantra 'Goosfrabaaa' under my breath over and over. Then, I shrugged it off and carried on being a happy-go-lucky student. It was only many years later that a niggling feeling began to resurface; akin to a cancerous tumour that gradually expands in your body, turning healthy optimistic cells into rotten 'doubters'. In hindsight, however innocent that comment seemed, it did the desired damage; it told me I would never be able to write like a native English speaker. Without going into great detail about my personal biography, I will divulge the fact that English is my third language. Throughout my young adult years, I constantly felt the need to prove that I was good enough. And having done that as a young adult, first by being accepted into a top sixth-form college, and later into Durham University, I had finally managed to put my demons to rest.

But as it turned out, the demons were still there, waiting for something to trigger them, and Mrs. Schumacher supplied it with pinpoint accuracy. It is quite possible that this trigger was the main factor that prevented me from writing this book earlier. Another reason might be the fact that there is a great chance of me being expelled from Germany, should this book ever get published. Taking Brexit into consideration, and the fact that I might become a persona non grata, there is a risk of my being denied a residency visa on the grounds of having an *anti-German* mindset. And, finally, the biggest paradox of all: twelve years in this country have wreaked an irreversible change on my mindset - slowly taking me from a British way of thinking to a German one. Thus, I'm beginning to think and reason like the Germans do. The transformation is slowly taking its toll, and thus, in a year's time, I probably won't be able to write this book at all. So let's get cracking, while I still can.

DISCLAIMER

Fadi is an international living in Germany. He has lived in Germany for fifteen years and experienced life as a fully integrated expat. His writing is intended as satire and outlines his experiences in Germany. No offence is intended. However, if you do take offence, you are either too sensitive, too German, or both.

Since this book is primarily aimed at expats, and more importantly written by an expat, the chapters are arranged in a quasi-chronological order of events, as would happen to a person who had just moved to Germany from another country. Just like a survival guide, the topics are written in order of importance. And thus, getting to know your surroundings, including your workplace and home environment, is an essential step to adapting to life in Germany. These sections are followed by chapters concerning the German language, food and leisure activities. Subsequently, you will get to a bit of information about German culture, history and religion — not every single item of importance, but just enough to be able to converse with people around you, and, more importantly, avoid being branded as an *ignorant foreigner*; a title which, actually, many expats are perfectly content with. In the latter chapters we round off with topics on dating, relationships and family life. And, finally, a concluding chapter brings everything together, comparing the *best* and the *worst* traits, in order to give the reader a (semi-)objective view of the Germans, and help them decide if Germany is really suited for them.

Chapter 1

At Home & In Your Living Quarters

Having finally accomplished your lifelong *dream* of moving to Germany — okay, that might be a bit exaggerated, but let's assume for now that this is actually how you feel — you find yourself immersed in new and exciting surroundings: the language, the culture, the people, the mentality, even the smell — everything is different. But before you can start exploring, you'll first need to sort out the basics — essential things you need to survive — like finding your nearest supermarket, working out your route to work with public transport, getting a sim card for your phone, or registering at the local government office. These things will occupy most of your time during your first few weeks in Germany. Undoubtedly, all of these new experiences will start to throw up a lot of questions, as you try to adapt to the way 'things are done' here. Some of these questions and problems will be relatively straightforward; others will be less simple; and a few things will make absolutely no sense at all. In order to give you – the expat — a bit of a head start, this chapter goes over a few of the things that it took me a while to get my head around when I first moved to Germany, in particular those that have an effect on your immediate surroundings.

Getting an apartment

One of the first things people need when they move to Germany is a room or an apartment. Depending on where you want to live, the task of getting a place can quickly become exhausting, almost like a full-time job. The cost of living obviously depends on which city you live in, and the neighbourhood. If you look further afield, you can easily find houses to rent for the same price as a two-bed apartment in Hamburg, Munich or Berlin. Most people who move to a new city in Germany tend to start out with just renting a furnished room, to give them some time to get settled, and to do some location scouting, before they zero in on exactly where they want to live and get searching for their own place.

Tenancy laws in Germany clearly favour the tenant, which is good news. They prevent the landlord from constantly putting up the prices for existing tenants. They also prevent landlords from evicting tenants for the sake of hiking up prices. This is illegal — the laws are clear about that. The only situation in which it is allowed is if the landlord intends to move into the place themselves, and even then they have to give at least three months' notice to the sitting tenants. This is the main reason why people in Germany tend to live in their apartments for very long periods, sometimes literally decades. When I was apartment-hunting in Berlin, I met some tenants who had been in their homes for over thirty years, and thus were still paying the same monthly rent as when they first moved in. In other words, they were living in a ninety-square-metre apartment paying just three hundred euros per month, while their newly moved-in neighbours were paying the going rate, roughly four times that.

Getting your own apartment in the city, as I found out, is a mammoth task, one which takes several months of viewings, sending documents to landlords, and praying that they will pick you. The thing that surprised me most was the sheer amount of paperwork I had to submit to the landlords - in advance of even attending the viewing. I was asked to provide an employment contract, a public indemnity, three months of bank statements, three months of wage slips, a CV with a photograph and even a motivational letter stating why I would make the perfect 'apartment candidate'. According to the various forums I visited as my desperation to find a place turned to despair, the perfect candidates were usually young couples, who both had permanent jobs. Couples with children were less desirable, and pets were outright banned. Amongst the most desired professions were civil servants, teachers, doctors, engineers and police officers. Apparently, the least desirable profession in the eyes of the landlord is a lawyer. It makes sense.

Then came the shock of the actual viewing. As it turned out, details about these are often posted publicly on the rental company's website, including the exact time and date. When I went to my first viewing, I was shocked to see no fewer than sixty people loitering next to the building entrance. All of them were interested in the apartment. "Bollocks," I thought to myself. "At this rate I'm never going to get a place of my own." Eventually, a man turned up and announced to everybody that he was from the rental company. He went up to the flat, and the hoard of hopefuls duly followed him. The apartment was already vacated: all of the furniture gone, the plaster and flooring ripped out. It was basically just a shell that was about to be renovated. I quickly realised that, compared to the other potential tenants, I had come completely unprepared. They all turned up with lists of questions, which covered everything from the type of flooring that was going to be put in and the specifics of the electrics, to the building's heating system and energy efficiency rating. They had brought their own tape measures and thermometers, apps measuring noise decibels from the outside, and even some other weird apparatus that apparently measured if the place was damp. I started to feel like a pupil who had turned up for a lesson, only to find out that there was a test for which everybody else had been avidly preparing, that I didn't know anything about.

Over the next weeks, and months, I went from viewing to viewing, repeating the same process over and over, handing in my documents and hoping they would pick me ahead of all the chirpy, smiling, young, civil servant couples. I must have seen close to fifty different apartments. After the first month, my standards dropped dramatically, and after the second month I was ready to live in a dog kennel, as long as it had my name on it and a patch of dirt where I could curl up for the night.

Into my third month of apartment-hunting, I got a tip off from a friend about a block of flats currently being renovated. It was relatively close to work, in an area with shops, parks and all the essential amenities. I went to the viewing (along with sixty other candidates), and to my delight, got a call from the rental office the following week, offering me one of the apartments. To say that I was over the moon would be a gross understatement. I didn't even care to ask which exact apartment they were referring to. I accepted blindly and hung up the phone.

Making German friends

Once you've found somewhere to live, it's time to sort out your social life.

Ever since I moved to Germany, most of the people I hang out with are expats just like me. Mostly either Scandinavian or native English speakers: Brits, Americans, Swedes, Egyptians, Norwegians and Danes. German people have only ever made up a modest proportion of my friendship group — somewhere between 0 and 5 percent, if we're talking specifics. There is a natural reason for that: expat people tend to hoard together with other expats. You meet them at your language school, or at the meetups organised in pretty much every major city in the *Bundesrepublik.* At work, you will cling on to the other international people and naturally you will have a lot more in common with them than the seasoned Germans. The language barrier is a given, but you'll find that German people are actually very good at speaking English (at least, they are in the major cities) and they will go out of their way to show off their language skills to you, however limited they may be, particularly at social events. This should come as a pleasant surprise, particularly to those who have experienced French hospitality — when it comes to speaking English.

Despite this fact (and the fact that I already spoke very good German when I arrived), I have always wondered why, in my nineteen years in Germany, I have only managed to truly bond with a few *natives*. If you pressed me for an answer, I'd tell you that I put it down to two cultural differences. The first one I tend to refer to as the ability to 'take the mickey' out of (make fun of) one's counterpart, which, as it turns out, is much more important to me than I had ever considered. The second one is a lot less complicated: I have come to the realisation that talking German while trying to relax is a bit like doing maths in your head while trying to go to sleep. In other words, it's like mixing oil with water (or chalk and cheese, as the British saying goes). Thus, unless German is your native tongue, speaking it will always involve that extra bit of effort on your behalf, putting you in a state of *not quite being yourself*, and preventing you from feeling completely at ease with your German counterparts.

That means you only have two options: the first one is to limit the amount of contact you have with German people and build your own expat circle (it sounds quite absurd, considering you live in Germany, but it is actually quite possible, if you so wish, and you'll come across plenty of other expats who are perfectly happy to pursue their social lives in this way). Or, the second option — and this is the one I would like to encourage you to pursue (although I can appreciate the irony of this remark, considering what's coming up in the rest of this book) — is to embrace the language, culture and people of this country, and have a real go at making some German friends. In reality, going down this route is the only option you have, if you intend to successfully integrate in the German society and *enjoy* living in this country.

So why is it so hard for some expats to bond with the Germans, you may ask? Taking this from an English-speaking point of view, I'd like to highlight a few differences in the way people go about *bonding* in Anglo-American and German cultures, as follows:

Piss-taking or *mocking* is an essential part of male bonding in Britain (since I don't really have any experience in 'female bonding', I'll just stick to male bonding). So, if you're talking to your British friend just after they've been for a haircut, you'd ask them whether they had an accident while mowing the lawn. Another example would be asking if your mate used all his savings on his new C&A jeans, or telling him that, with a face like his, his only chance of scoring would be in the Dark Room at Berghain[1]. In German, the word for piss-taking is *verarschen*, which can loosely be translated as 'arsing about'. Unfortunately, the word has a very negative connotation,

---

1   This, essentially German reference cites an underground club in Berlin, famous for its wild parties and sexual freedoms. *The Dark Room* refers to a room with no light that is a designated space where complete strangers have intercourse.

and anyone suspected of *taking the piss* will only invoke hostility, rather than smiles.

Only recently, I was at Hamburg airport going through security, and a very polite gentleman working on the x-ray scanner asked me to empty all my pockets into the tray, take my laptop out of its case, and place it in a separate tray. He had a facial expression I can only describe as that of someone who is really dying to go for a big *Thomas tit* (cockney rhyme slang for going for a number two), but can't because it isn't the end of their shift yet. He asked me if I had any liquids on me — basically the usual spiel you get at airport security that most of us have probably been through a gazillion times before. When he asked me to take off my top and my belt, I put on my usual cheeky smirk and asked if I was allowed to keep my underwear. His reaction was quite dramatic: he looked at me with hatred and shouted, *"Wollen Sie mich verarschen?"* — as in, "Are you taking the piss??" I was mortified. It made me feel as though I had really offended him, as though, instead of poking fun in a subliminal attempt to cheer him up, what I had actually asked him was, "Can I sleep with your sister?" Of course, in retrospect, he probably was just tired of hearing the same joke for the umpteenth time.

With that in mind, I've compiled the ten commandments of 'Dos and Don'ts', if you want to make any German friends. (Unfortunately I could only come up with eight, but ten sounds more meaningful).

The dos and don'ts if you want to make German friends

- Do not use wit or sarcasm; it will never be understood
- If you do tell a joke, be sure to say, "That was a joke," immediately after. Be prepared to explain the joke if they don't seem to get it.
- There is no friendly way of taking the piss out of Germans; just don't do it.
- A good conversation starter is to talk about your health problems, your doctor's appointment, or the latest insurance policy you have taken out.
- If somebody is telling you about how they had to call in sick and go to the doctor because they had a runny nose or a sore throat, do not — whatever you do — mock them. Be understanding and compassionate. Throw in words like, *"Ach du armer!"* (Poor you!) or *"Gute Besserung"* (Get well soon!)
- When another person is talking, be attentive and show empathy, for instance by mimicking their facial expressions. Paraphrase their responses when it's your turn, and never interrupt or interject when the other person is talking.
- When asked a question, be informative, precise, elaborate, and serious. Do not offer short or wishy-washy answers like, "Could be better" or "Yeah, alright".
- Make appointments with your friends, and be on time! I can't stress this one enough.

Going to the supermarket

I remember the first time I went to a supermarket in Hamburg, as most people remember the first time they drove a car, or the first time they went on a trip without their parents, or that time they fell off their bike. I can't really say if it was because of the psychological trauma it inflicted upon me, but I vividly remember every detail. Basically, it went something like this:

09:58 — Enter the supermarket.

10:02 — Some tw*t barges into me without saying anything. Does not apologise.

10:04 — Standing at the grocery section, contemplating whether my Macbook Pro needs another memory card update, and some douchebag reaches right across me, again without uttering a single word. Instinctively I turn and say, "Sorry", to which I get no reaction.

10:05 — Shop assistant ignores my attempts to get his attention because I can't find the dairy section. I could well be standing in one of the mazes hidden inside the Egyptian Pyramids, surrounded by ancient hieroglyphs, or teleported to another galaxy, and I would be equally lost.

10:08 — Yet another aimless walk around the shop without any luck.

10:10 — After walking three times through every aisle of the shop I finally manage to find milk, bread, some toilet paper, and something that looks like chicken breasts.

10:12 — I get in the queue and wait. A guy walks right past me and queues up beside an individual checkout. "How rude," I think to myself, making a mental note, but doing nothing.

10:13 — A woman walks right past me and does the same bloody thing. My head is about to explode, but this time I've learnt the lesson. I take a step forward into the left line and wait for my turn.

10:15 — I'm finally being served by the cashier, who looks at me with disgust and asks me which types of *'Brötchen'* (bread rolls) I've selected. The three rolls are in a see-through plastic bag. I shrug; my whole body takes the shape of a question mark. Apparently I am supposed to know exactly which type of bread roll I have selected (and there are at least twenty in the bakery section). I apologise profusely and promise to memorise the names for all the different types of *Brötchen* before my next visit. The annoyed cashier demonstratively looks through the list behind her till. At the same time, I can feel the aura of disapproval emanating from the people behind me in the form of a quiet, but distinct murmur.

10:17 — *"DREIZEHN NEUNZIG!"* the cashier barks at me. I produce the only bill I have in my wallet, which is a fifty euro note. As you can imagine, this doesn't go down well. I feel like Indiana Jones in the *Temple of Doom*, about to get discovered by the mob. Another step in the wrong direction, and I will be compromised. I will end up rotating on a skewer with an apple stuck in my mouth.

10:18 — The cashier rolls her eyes at me in disbelief, followed by a very long sigh, then takes my bill while muttering something under her breath.

10:19 — Again, I apologise, take my change, and make a dash for the exit without looking back, like the sole survivor of a zombie movie.

DIY Saturdays & Church Sundays

It's no secret that Germans like order and structure, and this mantra extends into pretty much every aspect of their daily lives. Since the supermarkets are closed on a Sunday (as is everything else, for that matter), most people do their family shopping on a Saturday — which is why you'll find it a most unpleasant experience, should you foolishly decide to venture into ALDI, EDEKA, or any other major supermarket chain on that day of the week. For people who do not like food shopping, there are options to get your groceries delivered, but Germans are not very keen on that, for some strange reason. Another favourite activity reserved for Saturdays is DIY and the ominous and unavoidable trip to the Baumarkt, which is where you get all your home supplies. There is a separate chapter dedicated to this later on.

As a foreigner, you need to know that DIY is not allowed on Sundays in Germany – by law — hence why the Sabbat is also known as a Ruhetag (quiet day). So things like drilling, mowing the lawn, vacuuming and even singing are prohibited. As you can imagine, Germans are very precise about these types of things, and they love making rules. Put two and two together, and voilà, you've got a list of rules of things you can and cannot do on a Sunday. So, for example, vacuuming is allowed but only if your vacuum cleaner produces sixty-five decibels of noise or less (no joke). Anything above that is out of the question. Whether or not you are allowed to wash your car (which you can only do at designated car wash places), is a rule that differs from federal state to federal state. Washing your clothes, on the other hand, is okay. I don't want to be the one to tell you, but ignoring these rules can cause a lot of agro with your neighbours. They might even call the Ordnungsamt (a regulatory body responsible for the upkeep of such regulations) on you, and they are entitled to do so.

As a rule of thumb, Sundays are reserved for *Sunday breakfast*, which must include certain things for it to qualify as such: at least two different types of bread rolls *(Brötchen)* and one type of sweet pastry like croissants; at least two types of savoury toppings like cheese, ham or salami and at least one sweet topping like marmalade or jam; sliced vegetables and, of course, coffee and tea. For most Christians, a trip to your local church is a compulsory activity on a Sunday, while others may choose recreational activities such as jogging, cycling, hiking, or long walks in the forest, basically anything that can be classified as exercise. In the afternoon, you usually have *Kuchenzeit* (cake time), spent with your family, inlaws, or friends. After your *Abendbrot* (dinner), watching an episode of *Tatort* is obligatory, to put the cherry on top of your perfect German Sunday. More on that later.

Thrifty Germans

In my younger days in Germany, when I used to go food shopping with my flatmates, I was often baffled by the thriftiness that possessed them. It's not that I'm throwing money around left, right and centre, constantly living it large. Not at all. However, in comparison to my German counterparts of the same age, I definitely was. To them, I was borderline *careless* with money. For example, if I picked up a packet of cheese that didn't have a red reduced sticker on it, I was promptly told to put it down. And if there was a similar item that was — let's say — seven cents cheaper in a supermarket a fifteen-minute walk from us, then it was always the obvious choice to go for the cheaper item there instead. Another example of my apparently cavalier attitude towards money: the cashiers at the supermarkets would never let you off if you turned up even one cent short of the sum required. I've tested this myself, and every time I was told to produce the missing *cent*. The truth is, Germans love saving money, and they love boasting about it too. Indeed, such a topic is very popular in all social circles, whether at work, in a pub, at home, or in any other setting. There is never a wrong time or place for this kind of a discussion. Germans are happy to discuss the money they have saved on car insurance, food shopping, gadgets, clothing, or even their last meal with friends. Incidentally, that last point deserves a special mention. If you find yourself dining with your friends or colleagues, it is very common to split the bill at the end, down to the very last cent. There won't be anybody saying, "Just give us a tenner mate" or "Let's just split it all equally" and definitely not, "Just buy us dinner next time." Instead, there will be a meticulous process of calculating how much each and every person owes, including the tip, followed by each individual paying separately to the waiter. If the staff are particularly useless, in some instances, you'd be expected to add the sums and pay together — one bill, that's how it works over here.

Once in a while, many German people deliberately forget their thriftiness for one evening, a weekend, or even a week, and that's when they go and *splash the cash*. The German term for this is *gönnen* — literally meaning, to *treat oneself*. I've seen this many times in my experience as a hotel musician. Couples would arrive for a weekend package at a five star hotel, the kind of place where a room without breakfast starts at about three hundred euros. They would wine and dine, cocktails, champagne, fancy dinner, the whole smorgasbord, and as the weekend progressed they would visit the spa, go for various massage treatments, do walks on the beach and so on and so forth. Others might *treat* themselves to a cruise, a holiday to Mallorca, or a skiing trip in the Alps. The principle is the same. It is quite common for the Germans to *reward* themselves for the hard work they do, and indeed, Germans do work a lot.

Pfand: Do not bottle it

Germany is a country obsessed with the environment, carbon footprints, and recycling. Perhaps only second to the Netherlands, Germany has one of the most sophisticated recycling systems in the world. For example, it was one of the first countries to introduce charges for the use of plastic shopping bags from the supermarkets, long before anyone else followed suit. The Bundesrepublik has always portrayed itself as being a pacemaker in matters like reducing carbon emissions, wind and solar power, renewable energy, and so on and so forth. But perhaps the most cunning invention that was introduced by Germany is Pfand (literally translatable as 'deposit', it is a system for recycling plastic bottles). It's simple enough: you pay an extra twenty-five cents at the shop for each drink in a plastic bottle (or eight cents for glass bottles), and, when you bring the empty bottles back, you get your money back. Simply deposit your empty bottles into one of the recycling machines, which you will find at pretty much all supermarkets, listen to that crunching sound it makes as your bottles are squashed down to the size of a coin, and presto! Once you get the hang of it, it becomes a bit of an obsession, so even if you buy a bottle of Coke at a football game, you hold on to it and take it home with you, because otherwise that's twenty-five cents you're throwing away! The most extreme case of this I've witnessed in public was at a classical concert venue: a guy was refused entry because he had an empty Coke bottle with him. He protested vehemently, shouting, "But it's *PFAND!*"[2]

The insurance obsession

Relatively recently, I ordered some cinema tickets online. Before the booking was finalised, I was taken to another page which asked me if I wanted to insure my tickets, which I found a bit absurd. Presumably, some people feel the need to take out insurance on cinema tickets which cost about nine euros each, in case they fall ill and can't fulfil their commitment.

---

2 If you'd like to know more about recycling in Germany, you could do some further reading on the https://www.nabu.de — the nature preservation society. What I learned there, was the fact that there are in fact two systems of recycling bottles: the so-called single use, and multiple use one. As the word suggests — single use are your cans of coke, and anything that can't be reused, while other plastic bottles can actually be used again, hence the term.

It's no secret that Germany is the most insured country in the world, statistically speaking, ranking even higher up than the USA. There is literally insurance for everything. It's no wonder that the Germans have incorporated insurance into their list of *acceptable small talk topics*. I can think of one incident that elucidates this better than anything else. I was playing football on an enclosed pitch next to a bike path, and at one point the ball was kicked over the fence. I went to fetch it and then kicked it back towards the pitch. The ball went up, then down, bouncing multiple times. Unfortunately, there was a female cyclist on the bike path. She saw the ball bouncing towards her and panicked, like a deer in the headlights, left, right, centre, wobbling back and forth. She didn't know where to go. As Murphy's law would have it, the ball ended up hitting the front wheel of her bike, square on, breaking her light — or at least knocking it off, slightly. It was almost as if the whole thing had happened in slow motion (if you've seen the steam-roller scene in *Austin Powers,* you'll know what I mean), or a deliberately and comically absurd fight scene in a movie. Call it what you like, the collision was inevitable.

I ran up to see if she was okay, which obviously she was, but, having seen the broken light, she immediately asked, *"Haben Sie Haftpflichtversicherung?"*

"What the heck is that?" I retorted.

What she had in fact asked was if I had any 'public liability insurance'. The German term is a compound of three words: *Haft, Pflicht* and *Versicherung.* Put them together and it's enough to make your tongue do a double knot. Your saliva will project ten metres forward as you attempt to pronounce it.

To Germans, the word is an institution in itself; a pillar upon which they identify themselves as *Germans*; a proud social common denominator — the German DNA, if you like. In other words, if Frank Schmidt is on holiday in Portugal, and feeling homesick, it is likely that he will find someone from his own country to talk to about *Haftpflichtsversicherung*. It's the perfect antidote to homesickness. The fact is, although public liability insurance is not mandatory in Germany, it may as well be, given how many people have it and swear by it.

Since then, I've witnessed many conversations like the one I had with the broken bike lady. If you have an accident, a break-in at home, your bike stolen, an emergency that cuts your holiday short, or literally anything that has not gone according to the *master plan*, be prepared for the fact that the first question anyone is going to ask you is if you are insured against whatever just happened. Paranoia, you might say? To anyone who is not from Germany, a definite yes. But to Germans, this is a simple fact of life. They hate surprises and unforeseen circumstances, things not going according to plan and things that happen — and I'm going to use the most blasphemous word in the German lexicon — *spontaneously*. Every German is constantly asking themselves, "What if?" And nothing would irk them more than a scenario in which that question remained unanswered.

"What happens if I fall over?"

"Do I have insurance that covers me?"

If you are reading this with scepticism, thinking, "Oh, this guy is just bitter," or "He's got a tiff with the Germans," you are more than welcome to put my hypothesis to the test. Next time you talk to a German person, throw in a couple of happy-go-lucky phrases like, "We'll see what happens," or "Let's play it by ear." You will immediately notice a reaction, which might be more or less visible, depending on the amount of *Germanness* the person opposite you is in possession of. But be assured you will get the reaction. It will be either in the form of immediate quick-fire questions demanding you explain what you mean, or there will be a long silence during which they display a confused expression on their face. Like that of a computer that has been fed a formula that contradicts itself, which it keeps trying in vain to compute. Eventually the mainframe caves in, and the CPU explodes from overheating.

In other words, everything must be logical and coherent, like a formula. A must equal B, and A plus B must equal C. There are no *if* formulas. This logical thinking is very closely related to the notion of control. Most Germans are obsessed with trying to control every part of their existence, and that ties in with their need to always see things through properly. In their defence: have you ever read the small print in an insurance contract? Probably not, but if you did, you'd find all sorts of nasty sentences that limit the insurer's accountability for things that you, as the insured person, probably take for granted. A good German person grows up with a mechanism that ensures they read the small print. This instinct is conditioned from a very young age. You'll have come across this reflex if you've ever visited an 'official' institution in Germany, be it a bank, a university, a tax office, or government office. If you forget something, or get some minute detail wrong, the first thing you'll hear is an accusation: "Did you not read the information on the website?" or "Did you not read the smallprint?"

This explains, at least in part, why this topic occupies so much time in Germany, whether at home, at the workplace, or during social gatherings. The average German person — depending on their age, of course — will have anywhere between nine and twenty different insurance policies attached to their name. Here is a list of most common ones:

- Public liability insurance *(Haftpflicht)*
- Car insurance
- Roadside cover
- Home insurance
- Travel insurance
- Sickness insurance
- Legal cover insurance *(Rechtschutz)*
- Bicycle theft
- Two types of pet insurance (if you have a dog, a cat, or a horse)
- Life insurance

And that's just the tip of the iceberg. All types of insurances have different premiums, which include or exclude a myriad of additional services. I've read through all of them and I can tell you that some of them border on the absurd. A good example is car insurance: if you inspect the cheaper premiums, you'll notice that — aside from the obvious things like a higher excess, third party coverage and no-claims protection in case of an accident — they also exclude things like 'being bitten by an animal', collision with a wild animal, hail and hurricane damage, quote protection, and the 24-hour accident hotline. To me, personally, the extra add-ons are not something I'm going to lose any sleep over, but rest assured — the Germans certainly will. For a nation that hates surprises and constantly asks itself *what if* questions, I suppose I can understand the constant worrying. I'm not liking them any more for it, however.

Below is a screenshot from a well-known comparison website in Germany — Check24.

It contains no fewer than eight main insurance headings and a whopping total of thirty-one different types of insurance available. For those readers who do not speak a word of German, I've taken the liberty in translating them into English. I have to admit, even after my nineteen years in this country, I still struggled to identify some of the types of insurance on offer and had to look them up first. For example; *death benefit insurance* covers your funeral costs, and a *Heilpraktiker und Brille* insurance will cover the costs of your homeopathy therapist and your optometrist, which are not covered by your normal health insurance.

Fig. 1 shows different Insurances available from the Check 24 website.

Auto & Fahrzeuge	Haftpflicht & Haus	Tiere	Risiko & Vorsorge
Kfz-Versicherung	Privathaftpflicht	Hundehaftpflicht	Risikolebensversicherung
Motorradversicherung	Hausratversicherung	Hundekrankenversicherung	Unfallversicherung
Moped oder E-Scooter	Wohngebäudeversicherung	Katzenversicherung	Berufsunfähigkeit
Schutzbrief/Automobilclub	Neubauversicherung	Pferdehaftpflicht	Grundfähigkeitsversicherung
Fahrradversicherung	Handyversicherung	Pferde-OP-Versicherung	Sterbegeldversicherung

Recht & Reise	Krankenversicherung	Krankenzusatz & Pflege	Altersvorsorge
Rechtsschutzversicherung	Private Krankenversicherung	Zahnzusatzversicherung	Rentenversicherung
Reiseversicherung	Gesetzliche Krankenkassen	Krankenhauszusatz	Sofort-Rente
Konto-Schutzbrief		Heilpraktiker und Brille	
		Pflegeversicherung	

Cars & Vehicles

- Car insurance
- Motorcycle insurance
- Moped or e-scooter
- No claims protection / automobile club
- Bike insurance

Liability & House

- Personal liability
- Household insurance
- Homeowners' Insurance
- New build insurance
- Cell phone insurance

Animals

- Dog liability
- Dog health insurance
- Cat insurance
- Horse liability
- Horse surgery insurance

Risks & Precautions

- Term life insurance
- Accident insurance
- Occupational disability
- Basic skills insurance
- Death benefit insurance

Law & Travel

- Legal protection insurance
- Travel insurance
- No claims protection

Health insurance

- Private health insurance
- Statutory health insurance

Health supplement & care

- Dental insurance
- Hospital addition
- Homeopathy and glasses
- Care insurance

Retirement planning

- Pension insurance
- Immediate pension

The walk of shame

If you live in Germany, there are three cardinal sins that you should never commit:

1.   Talk about the war in a social context
2.   Tell inappropriate jokes at work
3.   Cross the traffic lights on red

The first and second points are covered in detail later in this book, but in this chapter we shall devote our attention to the third option — the red man.

In a rule-obsessed country like Germany, breaking the rules in private is embarrassing enough, but doing it in public is akin to committing murder in broad daylight - in front of others. This even extends to crossing the road on red. In fact, I'm pretty sure that, in the German translation of the Bible, another sentence has been added to the list of ten commandments: "Thou shall not cross the red light (lest ye shall be banished to hell for eternity)." That's how serious this is.

For example, if you've ever been to the centre of Hamburg, you'll probably have walked down the street that's home to the shortest pedestrian crossing in Germany (possibly in the entire world). It's located opposite the Alex Cafe on Jungfernstieg. It only takes three large steps to get from one side to the other, and yet, you'll find that there are traffic lights on both sides of the crossing. If you're in town on a Saturday, you will undoubtedly witness the most bizarre spectacle of all, one that epitomises the German rule-abiding culture as good as anything else: crowds of people waiting patiently for the green light on both sides of the crossing. It is hardly relevant if there are any cars passing or not — those are the rules, so you must follow them. If you dare to step off the 'kerb' and defy centuries of rule-making, you will immediately feel a sharp burning sensation on the back of your head. This is the accumulated effect of hundreds of eyes boring into you; a molotov cocktail consisting of disbelief, embarrassment (on your behalf) and sheer shock, which ultimately turns into despising your very existence.

The Germans have a term for this; it's called '*Fremd-schämen*' — being embarrassed for somebody else. And one sure way of experiencing this is to jaywalk. If you want to elevate your status to 'enemy of the state', then you could try crossing on red while there are kids present. Just make sure you're prepared for the onslaught of abuse shouted in your direction, along the lines of *"ES IST ROT!!!"* (It's red!), or the more lecture-like alternative: "What kind of example do you think you are setting to the children, you antisocial so and so?"

For a long time — I must confess — I continued to cross on red purely out of conviction. My instinct told me, if there are no cars, then there is no reason why you shouldn't be able to cross. But that was a long time ago. Nowadays, far from being a reformed character, I find myself jaywalking with a lot more purpose, a certain feeling of defiance — to separate myself from the masses, to wave my proverbial British flag, and to stick my middle finger in their German faces, in a "F*ck you, I'm British!" kind of way. I didn't say I was proud of myself. More recently, I've gradually come to understand that even the Germans themselves have certain issues with the 'red man'. This is particularly true of the younger generation — those who have travelled abroad and seen the reality of the 'red light rule' elsewhere. Or — to put it bluntly — the complete disregard for it. Every now and then, you see a couple of Germans sneak across the pedestrian crossing on red. However, they always leave a palpable trail of guilt and shame behind them, like a red flag. There is a meme about this:

Two men stand next to each other at a pedestrian crossing. It's red, there are no cars, and it's midnight. A speech bubble appears above their heads. The text is identical and it reads: "If only the other guy wasn't here right now."

Whichever way you twist it — there is no easy way to go about it. You either give in, or you don't. Since becoming a teacher, I've cut down considerably on jaywalking. After all, I'm a civil servant now and thus I should be the embodiment of a model citizen. One fine day, one of my pupils saw me crossing on red, and I was *mortified*. He stood on the opposite side and glared at me in disbelief. For a moment, I wasn't sure how to respond, but managed to get my composure back and told the pupil that I could see into the future, which was why I crossed earlier. Unsurprisingly, the answer left him very puzzled. Either way, it gave me just enough time to swiftly turn the corner, and get out of his sight.

Here's a quick comparison of different logic when it comes to traffic rules:

British logic:
Question: Is it green?
→ Yes, then look right, walk to the middle, look left.
→ No, then look if there are any cars on the right, if not you're good to go.

Question: What if a car runs through a red light?
Answer: Well they do that anyway, so you've got to watch out all the time.

German logic:
Question: Is it green?
⟶ Yes, then you're free to walk!
⟶ No, then you must wait for green!
Question: What if a car runs through a red light?
Answer: Well, if it runs through red and hits me, I will be in the right, and the driver will be in the wrong, which means I will win the insurance claim.

Italian logic:
Question: Is it green?
Answer: What traffic light?

Going to the *Baumarkt*

I've never pretended to be skilful at DIY, and so I've always had to rely on the *professionals* to do the job of fixing stuff around the flat. Okay, this is not quite true. When I was in my twenties, and thought I knew everything and could do anything I put my hands to, I did my fair share of *trying* to fix stuff around the flat. More often than not, I ended up failing miserably. I'm even talking about simple things like painting the walls. Before I embarrass myself further by divulging such stories, I do have to mention the fact that Germans love their DIY. Going to the Home Depot store, known as the *Baumarkt,* is one of their favourite things to do on a Saturday. (In Germany, *Baumarkt* is to Saturday as church is to Sunday). To me, the experience of going to the *Baumarkt* is about as pleasurable as going to the dentist to get a tooth pulled out, or spending my day doing taxes. You get the gist. Let's start by examining why the Germans love it so much.

In Germany, tenants are allowed to carry out small cosmetic renovations on their dwelling — be it a flat or a house — provided that they return it to its original state when they vacate the premises at the end of their tenancy. Thus, if you so wish, you could paint the walls black, hang *Avant Garde* paintings, put up shelves, or even install an entirely new kitchen. Actually, the kitchen is very often a necessity, since a lot of flats do not have them when the tenant first moves in (or floors, or light fittings, for that matter). This is, in fact, is the reason many people find themselves at the *Baumarkt* on a Saturday morning.

To qualify for a visit to the *Baumarkt*, one must first 'graduate' from the University of DIY. If you are foolish enough to think that you can just stroll in, report to the information desk as a complete novice (read, *idiot*) and have a friendly employee sort you out with everything you need while you pick out wall colours and sip on a chai latte like they do in the adverts — well, to put it mildly, you're wrong! I've made that mistake, and had to learn it the hard way. First of all, you have to get your head around all the correct terminology — by which I mean the names of every possible item you might need to complete your task, including, but not limited to, the exact type of plywood you need, the exact type of appliance you should use it with, the exact type of screw, the exact type of wall and the exact measurements of your walls. Failure to get these details right will leave you blank-faced, quickly becoming overwhelmed by all the terminology that is being rapid-fired at you. You'll begin to sweat. You'll stutter. Then you'll probably mumble something along the lines of, "Oh, I didn't know", which will confirm the assistant's suspicion that you're a complete idiot.

Even if you pass Stage 1 and learn all the necessary terminology like *'Hohlraumdübel'*, or *'Federklappdübel'*, as well as the exact size of the hole you're facing and therefore the size of wall plug you need, you are still a long way away from 'mission complete'. You've merely passed to Stage 2.

To complete Stage 2, you need to successfully get a person to help you — and finding an employee in a building as huge as the *Baumarkt* is about as rare as finding a polar bear in the desert. If you actually manage to locate one, chances are he or she will be busy helping somebody else, and you will be forced to hover by them, like a vulture, waiting for the exact moment the other customer finishes and you can pounce on your prey. You'll have no more than a split-second to get their attention before someone else does. Even if on the inside you're screaming, you need to remain calm and, stepping firmly towards them, say *"Entschuldigung"* as loudly as you possibly can without shouting. If you naïvely believe that standing in their line of sight with a lame smile on your face is going to do the trick — well, my friend, you've never experienced German customer service and you'd be just as well off lighting a campfire right there in the middle of the store to get their attention. Another novice mistake expats like me often make is trying to stop an employee while they are busy helping somebody else. This will guarantee you the same reaction as if you had just stopped a stranger in the street asking for money. Best case scenario, they'll just ignore you. But if you're not so lucky, they might bark something at you to the tune of, "Can't you see I'm with a customer right now!?" Your natural reaction will be to apologise, and go hide somewhere in the corner of this massive complex.

All of this explains why, after countless attempts, I decided DIY was not for me and that the best way of solving any issues would be to call my landlord and ask them to get things fixed. After all, in the rental agreement there is a whole list of things that *must* be fixed by the landlord in case they are faulty. The only difficult thing is getting your wording right to make it sound like *their* problem. But, once that is done, you can rest assured that someone is going to call you to make an appointment to get it sorted. That is one comforting thing about living in Germany. Once it's written in black and white, then it's the law, and not adhering to the law, or worse, breaking it, is the most un-German thing anyone can do.

One fine day, I had a visit from the company that was supposed to fix up a tiny part of the ceiling that had previously leaked and now needed repainting — a job that would have literally taken two minutes, but I had no desire to get the paint from the *Baumarkt* myself. So I called the landlord. To my amusement, two people turned up. They stood in the bathroom for half an hour staring at the ceiling. Then, one of them got up on a chair to paint, while the other stood next to him with his hand on the chair. He was presumably making sure it didn't fall, but since the chair only went up to knee height, it was about as useful as propping up a tree. After they had finished painting, I asked if they could fix the same type of problem in the guest toilet, but was summarily rebuffed and told that I would have to make another appointment with the office for that. Marvelous, I thought to myself, this is what 'creating jobs' is all about.

Indeed, one of the things the Germans are really good at is creating employment. And this was a sterling example of that. Why give *one* task to somebody when you can create *five*, and why give that task to one person, when you can get five people to do the same thing. It's pure economics. We'll look at this in more detail later on.

Going to the government offices

Germany is one of the most bureaucratic countries in the world — Fact! Every aspect of your life in Germany is ultimately connected to a government office somewhere down the line, be it the passport office to get your residence permit, the local driving licence authority for your driving licence, the housing department, education, health, death and taxes - you name it. Everything imaginable will inevitably have a department connected to it, so if you want to settle down in the *Bundesrepublik,* you must come to terms with this, and it's not going to be easy.

To compound your misery as a foreigner, you will soon find out that every department contains a myriad of sub departments, and in turn these are divided into even more compounds, offices, corridors, booths, each and every one with its own area of *responsibility*. The tricky part is finding out who does what — and do not expect any help in figuring that out. Good luck!

To illustrate my point, I've included below a screenshot of a list of appointments, taken from the website of the transport department at my local governmental office. You are required to select the reason for your visit from this list — even though to the naked eye many of the options look pretty much the same. Do not make a novice mistake of selecting something that looks *more or less* accurate, because if you do that, you run the risk of being promptly turned away. No pleading, arguing or crying will help you. You'll have no choice but to go back home and make another appointment, one that exactly matches the reason for your visit. This also applies if you go without an appointment.

Fig. 2 Screenshot taken from the motor agency appointment page

erminvereinbarung:

Wählen Sie zunächst eine Dienstleistungsgruppe aus:

Antragsabgabe durch Fahrschulen (Barzahlung)

Bewohnerparken

Führerschein: Allgemeine Dienstleistungen

Führerschein: Neuerteilung nach Entzug

Führerschein: Spezielle Dienstleistungen

Kfz-Zulassung (Abmeldung und Adressänderung) online im Internet oder per E-Mail

Kfz-Zulassung (Abmeldung, Kurzzeitkennzeichen und mehr)

Kfz-Zulassung (Anmeldung, Umschreibung und mehr)

Rote Kennzeichen (Dienstleistungen aller LBV-Standorte)

Rote Kennzeichen (Dienstleistungen nur in HH-Nord)

Rote Kennzeichen (neue Fahrzeugscheinhefte, alle LBV-Standorte)

Fahrlehrerwesen

Source: https://www.lbv-termine.de/LBV

Of course, this is a *German governmental office*, so there's no option but to speak German, but to be kind I've translated the options for you. The tick box options are as follows, from top to bottom:

- Application by driving schools (cash payment)
- Residence parking permit
- Driver's license: General services

- Driver's license: Redistribution after withdrawal
- Driver's license: Special services
- Car permit (deregistration and change of address) online on the internet or by e-mail
- Car permit (deregistration, short-term identification and more)
- Car permit (registration, re-registration and more)
- Red license plates (services of all LBV locations)
- Red license plates (services only in HH-North)
- Red license plate (new vehicle license plates, all LBV locations)
- Driving instructor matters

Last week, I got a fist full of German bureaucracy smacked in my mouth, and it was quite an ordeal — not so much for myself, but for my wife. The whole reason for going there was to get a residence permit renewed. As a South African national, my wife has already been in Germany for a year. Unaccustomed to the German system, she was already freaking out a week before our appointment. However, being a trained lawyer, she prepared as best as she could, spending days photocopying the necessary documents and endlessly checking over the list of stuff she was supposed to bring with her. She even copied the stuff that I was supposed to bring with me, like my passport and the rental agreement — just in case. 'Freelance musician' is never a great title to have on your job description. This is particularly the case when going to the banks to ask for a loan, or to any institution where your income to expenditure ratio is of importance. And, in this particular case, it was essential.

Due to the coronavirus restrictions, the office was by appointments only. The sterile, spacious waiting room was full of empty chairs, with every second chair taped up in order to maintain the social distancing rule. After waiting for less than five minutes our number was lit up on the board, and we proceeded to room number 22. A heavy-set case worker in his mid-thirties with a full hipster beard and glasses was typing away at his desk, and without so much as moving an eyebrow, he spoke to us in a calm, controlled, firm manner — one that has been instilled into his DNA after years of working for the state. He spoke fast with very little intonation, and in German, of course: "And what are you here for?" *Gulp!* This was enough to set the tone for the meeting, and immediately my seventeen years of experience in Germany told me that this was going to be a tooth and nail battle.

A common misconception often held by expats in Germany is the idea that the first and foremost prerogative of government employees is to help the country's residents. If you use that as a logical starting point for all your deliberations then you've already lost the battle. In actual fact, at the very top of their list is the oath to preserve and uphold the law and the legislation of the *Bundesrepublik,* its core values, and the wellbeing of its citizens. Carefully note the order in which these words are written. The state and its laws come first and second, followed by its citizens.

Trying to be as calm as I could, I explained what we had come for, and put the pile of documents, neatly stacked, on the table. I also explained that my wife spoke very little German, and begged his understanding. The case worker didn't say a word, and instead began examining the documents carefully, his gaze flicking rapidly between the pile and his computer screen. He then turned to me and said that he needed a different photo of my wife. According to him, the one we gave him was identical to the one used on her old residence permit. Having examined the website and every single line of its font size ten print, I retorted that the website stated the photo can be as old as twelve months. To this, he responded that the information on the website was out of date. End of argument. Whichever way you twist it, you lose. Trying to use logic and reason will get you nowhere. The natural thing would be to think how absurd this is, for, if you can't get the correct information on the website, then how on earth are you supposed to figure this out?! At that moment, the case worker sensed for the first time that he might have gone too far and pointed us in the direction of a photo booth, which, luckily, was located on the premises. However, this particular gambit did not end there, as my wife, having understood what the problem was, protested, pointing out that indeed the photo in question was not the same: her hair was clearly a different length. She had only had the photo taken in February for her driving license, thus it could not be more than six months old.

Having realised his mistake, he eventually conceded, but, without apologising or acknowledging this, he simply moved onto the next part — the integration course. He asked for evidence that this had been completed. I said that we didn't have any evidence, after which a long pause ensued. He then said that having a certificate of completion was a prerequisite for getting a residence permit. My facial muscles tightened, but I knew that information wasn't correct, so I calmly rebuffed his attack by saying that only an unlimited visa requires the certificate. And, since my wife was applying for a three-year permit, she was not required to provide the course certificate. He left the room — probably to confirm with his colleague — and returned confirming my statement, once again, *apology accepted.*

A little note about the Anglo-Saxons:

In situations where people sit around and wait in silence, the most natural thing for an Anglo-Saxon would be to try to form a bond between oneself and the person on the opposite side. They try to establish a friendly rapport, lighten the mood, tell a joke, ask about the weather, football, really anything to break the ice and the uncomfortable situation they find themselves in. If this is you, then you must summon all your self-control and resist the urge to do anything of the sort. As you will soon come to realise (and we will discuss this at length in the next chapter), Germans aren't big on small talk. So the German civil servant will see this mindless chatter as a nuisance, an attempt to distract him from his perilous and important task, and this will cause the opposite effect of the one you intended. You've been warned. Now back to the story.

It was quite apparent that the civil servant assigned to us was displeased at not being able to unravel his victims to the point of agony and despair, but he did have one more trick up his sleeve. The final attack — the winner-takes-it-all kind of round — was the financial statement. He spent the next ten minutes asking various questions and setting various traps, just to see if his victims would react. In most cases, people do not expect an ambush and begin to panic, wondering what is going to happen if they do not get the residence permit, the choices they are left with, and the worst-case scenarios. However, in cases like these, you need to be like a defendant in a courtroom — maintain your calm composure — and be prepared for an onslaught from the prosecutor. The last thing you want is to show that you are affected by this, go on the defensive, or worst of all — get emotional and start babbling at random, clutching at straws.

After typing furiously on his computer for several minutes, he looked over and said that the numbers didn't add up, and that based on the financial information we had provided, he would not be able to issue a permit. BAM! There it was, the German Luftwaffe had delivered its final blow, and the effect tore through my poor wife's nervous system. She was visibly shell shocked. In her mind, she was already sitting on the repatriation flight to South Africa, saying goodbye to her husband. Her German adventure had come to an abrupt end.

A lot of people would have argued, in view of the fact that we were then sitting in the middle of a global pandemic, that perhaps the financial situation should be reassessed, and that it would be a bit rich for the government to deport people in such tough times. But this means absolutely nothing to a case worker, whose prime objective — as we have described above — is to preserve the German law and act upon it. My response was calm and friendly. I offered to show him my bank statements, which proved we had enough money to sustain ourselves for the duration of the residence permit, i.e. the next three years. Game, set and match! He looked at the statements and then began typing again without uttering a single word. Another five minutes passed, an eternity. A denied application would mean that we would have a week to appeal, would have to cancel our holiday, instead spending that time visiting the various *Amts*, and filling out paperwork until our fingers bled.

To our relief, the case worker confirmed the amount was sufficient (in actual fact it was more than ten times sufficient), and that a permit would be issued. All that was left was to pay the admin fee and get as far away from that place as possible. My wife told me on the way out that she felt like drinking a whole bottle of vodka. To add insult to injury, she also told me that the case worker actually spoke perfect English, having conversed quite fluently with her after the meeting had ended. *Welcome to German bureaucracy*, I thought to myself.

Dos and Don'ts:

- Do not, under any circumstances, resort to jokes, irony, or — worse — sarcasm. This will be seen as a direct attack on the person opposite you and they will do everything in their power to make your time there as miserable as possible.
- Make sure that you've read literally everything about the subject ahead of your appointment, and by that I do not only mean the official information on the government website, but also the various expat forums on the internet.
- Make sure you're familiar with the vocabulary and the jargon relevant to your case. A word like *Aufenthaltserlaubnis* is only the beginning of your vocab list. Also consider any compound words ending with *–bescheinigung, –nachweis, –bestätigung* and *–titel*, whose meanings will torment you during your many sleepless nights ahead of your appointment.
- Remember, the people at the government offices are not *intrinsically* there to help you. Do not expect them to empathise with you, or put themselves in your shoes.
- Always use a formal address to the case worker — the *Sie* form (more on this in a later chapter). It doesn't matter if they are younger than you, or if they are wearing shorts and t-shirt with the words *counterstrike* written on the front.[3] Remember, they have been trained to keep a distance from their clients.

---

3   A popular first person shooter game that every millennial male has spent their youth playing.

Driving a car in Germany

Driving a car in Germany can be extremely satisfying, fun even. Indeed, virtually no other place in the world has motorways with no speed limit (except maybe the Isle of Man, my editor tells me). In Germany, famously, the motorway is known as the *Autobahn,* an invention that is often erroneously credited to an infamous Austrian bloke, who went by the first name of Adolf, but that's beside the point. Driving in a German city is a whole different kettle of fish. Depending on where you live, some cities can be really chaotic and particularly difficult to navigate in a car, but we'll get to that in a bit. If you got your driving license in any country other than Germany, you need to be aware of the different driving rules here, or rather the difference in their *interpretation*. Let's take a look at some of the more unusual German driving quirks.

Honking the horn: It still drives me insane every time a car honks at me, particularly at a traffic light. The thing you need to understand is that Germans are used to people honking at them, and they will do the same unto others. There are several reasons Germans turn to honking their horns. Below I've listed some of the most common ones:

- If someone waits one nanosecond too long after the light has turned green.
- If another car has just barged in front of them, from another lane.
- If a car on the left won't let them into their lane, as per the German merging rule.[4]
- If a pedestrian runs across the road.
- If someone is driving at 49kmph in a 50 zone.

Blocking the inside lane: This one applies to cities in particular. Be it delivery vans, trucks, postal vans, or

---

4   German merging rule goes by the principle of one in one out, i.e. if suddenly two lanes turn into one, a car in the 'closed' lane has the right to barge into your lane without your acknowledgement. If you ignore the rule and don't let them in, be prepared to get an angry honk from them.

even normal cars, nobody will so much as blink an eye if a car suddenly decides to stop, put its hazard lights on, and do whatever they like at the side of the road.

Cyclists: Germany is a very green country, and the German government has made a great push to make their cities cycle-friendly. This primarily involves reconfiguring city infrastructure to make space for bike lanes on roads. Granted, this is fabulous for cyclists, and for the environment; however, for drivers, it adds another hazard they need to look out for, particularly when turning right into a sidestreet. Quite recently, some cities have even banished cars from their city centres, in a bid to go completely *car-free*.

The Autobahn: The thing to remember is that, on German motorways, speed is king. In other words, the one who drives the fastest has the right of way. Many drivers take this as a welcoming *carte blanche*, and you will inevitably see German cars whizzing past you at phenomenal speeds. But to many others, this can be quite an ordeal, particularly when someone is sitting right on your proverbial arse, wanting to pass. The thing to remember is that the yield rule applies to the middle lane too, so if somebody is driving faster than you in the middle lane, you are expected to yield into the outer lane. Remember, *hogging* the middle lane is frowned upon by Germans, and you will most likely feel their sentiment by seeing the front bumper of their car up close in your rear-view mirror.

Turning left at junctions: Probably the most confusing and frightening experience that you'll have as a driver in Germany is turning left at a junction. To understand why, you'll need to firstly get a bit of background information on Germany. Whereas the Anglo Saxons solved the junction problem with roundabouts, the Germans were relatively late to incorporate this concept into their traffic system. What you'll more commonly find is the so-called *square box* — basically, an intersection involving people travelling in four different directions. To turn left, a car must proceed to the middle of the junction, turn left slightly, and then wait for a gap in the oncoming traffic that allows them to turn into the adjacent road. The thing that makes many drivers a little uncomfortable: anyone in the oncoming traffic who wants to turn left will basically do the same as you, effectively stopping head-to-head with your car.

Driving in cities: If you want to put your driving skills to the ultimate test, then Berlin is the place to be. No other city in Germany is so chaotic and unpredictable as the capital. As a driver, you need to be constantly vigilant and aware of everything happening around you. This includes roadworks, traffic lights, changing lanes, turning left at road junctions, pedestrians, suicide cyclists, and, as if that isn't enough, you also need to look out for *Turkish* BMW drivers.[5]

---

5   This is a local saying, if a little xenophobic. It refers to young inexperienced drivers full of testosterone, usually of migrational background, ragging the hell out of top range BMWs.

Conclusion: Despite crazy speeds on *Autobahns*, Germans take their road safety very seriously, enjoying some of the lowest accident rates in Europe. You might think the drivers are rude and impatient for honking at you, but that's just a German thing. In reality, drivers tend to be very courteous, always letting you into the main lane, and patiently waiting for you while you're trying to parallel park on a busy street. They follow the rules to the letter of the law — hardly surprising — and they expect the same of you, or else they will blow their German horn at you. Have a nice drive.

Phoning customer service
(and why it's not such a good idea)

If you've had a bad day at work and you want to come home and relax, there are several things you could do. You could, for example, listen to Daniel Powter's one-hit-wonder *Bad Day*, or you could take a relaxing bath — provided you are privileged enough to have one. You could do many different things which involve various degrees of enjoyment.

One thing is not on that list: phone your phone company (or for that matter, any other customer service number located in Germany). In general, dealing with what passes for 'customer service' in Germany is the least desirable activity I can think of — outdone only by things like taking a number two in an airport toilet, or taking apart a blocked drainpipe in the kitchen. In this day and age, with the emergence of technology, help-bots, and re-al-time chat assistants offered by all major corporations, people are generally reluctant to pick up the phone, espe-cially to dial some 0800 number, posed with the prospect of being in a *queue* and talking to a complete *stranger*. To elaborate further, let's have a reality check: nobody calls anyone anymore. If you want to get in touch with your mates, you WhatsApp them, or voice-note them. This is particularly true of millennials. If a phone rings, this gen-eration does not have a clue what to do.

My point is — these recent technological develop-ments have fundamentally altered human behaviour and thus become habitual. Subsequently, they have had a di-rect effect on the world of business. In fact, most custom-er-friendly companies have embraced the changes and adapted to them, offering alternate options to customers, because they "still view happy customers as being quin-tessential to a successful business." Alas, these business practices do not apply in Germany — especially not to the large multinationals. "What a shame", as Gordon Ram-sey would say. Indeed, to put it mildly, Germany lags be-hind other countries when it comes to customer service. If I were to give it world ranking, I would probably put it somewhere between 190th and 192nd place (out of 195 —

smirk).

So, what is it exactly that is so bad with the German customer service?

To answer this question with an example, I have included a transcript of my most recent encounter with an employee at a car insurance company. I've added annotations to explain how each point contributed to my total psychological meltdown. If you'd like to read the interaction in detail, you can refer to the transcript below. If, however, you have an aversion to frustrating situations and wilfully unhelpful people, you can skip to the next chapter.

Reason for calling: I was at the department of motor and traffic — known as the *Verkehrsamt* — to register a car, but couldn't get a permanent registration due to the fact that some documents were missing. So, instead, I had to get a provisional registration to cover me for a period of five days. I needed to call the insurance company to get that sorted. Little did I know what I was letting myself in for (cue ominous music).

Literal Transcript:
Call agent: Hello, Smith — my name, how may I help?
Me: Hello, Gaziri — my name, and I need to get provisional short-term insurance for my car.
Call agent: Do you have a policy with our company?
Me: I did two years ago, but not anymore.

Call agent: Did you have a policy with anyone else in those two years?

Me: No, I didn't have a vehicle.

Call agent: Ok.

Me: …

Call agent: What is the VIN number of the vehicle?

Me: Is that the long number beginning with letters?

Call agent: It's also known as the type label (Typenschild) number.

Me: Ahm, I'm not sure what number that would be, I only have the long number here on the piece of paper.

Call agent: In that case we can't proceed.[6]

Me *(Slightly put off by that answer)*: Okay, I think I got it, it's W - A - U…

Call agent: I said it's NUMBERS only!

Me *(Breaking into a sweat)*: Ah okay, so I've got a number, but it's only zeros.

Call agent: That is what I need. It's zeros because it was most likely reset.

Me: Ah, I see.

Call agent: What's the number?

Me: Well, we just established it's zeroed out, didn't we?

Call agent: Ah yes, that is correct!

Call agent: What is the make of the car?

Me: Audi A3, Limousine

Call agent: What was the year of first registration?

---

6   I've heard this ominous phrase so many times in the past. In German — "Da kommen wir nicht weiter". It means, "We can't help you", and once you get to the stage where you hear it used in a conversation, you know that you're really 'up against it'.

Me: I think 2016.

Call agent: What is the size of the engine?

Me: Let me check, I think it's 1.8.

Call agent: No, I can't find a vehicle on the system with those specifications.

Me *(Feeling like an army cadet being drilled by the lieutenant, nervous sweating, and dreading the next question)*: So what do you suggest?

Call agent: There's nothing I can do, unless you give me correct information!

Me *(Fuming, pushed to the point that would stretch the patience of even a Zen Buddhist, but not prepared to ruin a whole day's work, so summoning all the patience I have left)*: Okay, so try putting in 2015 as the year of first registration.

Call agent: No, that doesn't come up with anything on the system either.

Me *(Noticing how the customer has now become the agent)*: Ok, how about putting in 1.79 as the engine size?

Call agent: Okay, we have the vehicle on our system.

I'm going to spare you the rest of this conversation, but you get the idea. I guess the point I'm trying to make here is twofold: Firstly, in Germany you have to be an expert in everything, if you want to get anywhere. And secondly — there is a break somewhere in the relationship between the large-scale companies and the end customer. A missing link, if you like, or perhaps even lack of understanding that the customers are the ones who ultimately *pay your wages*. In the next chapter I'll examine it from the other *end of the schtick*, as we delve into the German workplace.

In most first-world countries, and even in economically developing countries, if you're unhappy with the person on the other end of the phone, you can ask to speak to a supervisor, which is to say you've had enough of incompetence of the customer service agent, and you want to push the matter further up the food chain. If that's your expectation, then you're in for a real shock! In Germany there *is* no other level. The buck stops with the call agent, and if you feel that you're getting nowhere, you have no option but to put the phone down and spend the next thirty minutes or so looking through the guidelines for a written complaints procedure on the company's website. On a positive note, once you've filled out an online complaints form, rest assured, somebody will get in touch with you sooner or later (with emphasis on the latter).

A word of advice: If you decide to complain to somebody on the receiving end, do not use polite allusions, and soft conditional verbs, by which I mean phrases like 'might be' or 'could have'. Instead, be as strongly worded as you possibly can. Use phrases like *"Das geht gar nicht!"* (That's absolutely not on), or *"Wollen Sie mich verarschen?"* (Are you taking the piss?), both of which Germans love using in such situations.

If you come from a country like the US, the UK, Australia, South Africa, Eastern or Central Europe, Russia, or

The customer is not king:
Just accept it!

Asia, and, especially from the Middle East or the UAE, you will find it extremely difficult to adapt to the way people speak to you in Germany, especially in a customer service type of conversation; be it at a supermarket, on the phone, in shops, or in restaurants, basically in any setting where you pay money to the other person in exchange for them doing something for you. The reason for this is that, back in your native country, you as a customer have become accustomed to set phrases like 'The customer is king' and 'The customer is always right'. You have to understand that, in this country, this is probably the biggest misconception you have brought along with you. Thus, the *fault* is not with Germany, but with your own expectations.

But don't be disheartened; there is a way to remedy this, although it might take a long time. Do the following:

- Repeat the mantra to yourself over and over again: "The customer is not king. The customer is always wrong."
- Keep repeating these words until you finally get over your snobby expectation of being treated like a paying customer.

This is how I became accustomed to "customer service" in Germany - albeit only after fifteen years of living here. Here's one final strategy that I've found very useful: try taking a different approach. Imagine you're a beggar on the street, having just stopped a complete stranger and asked them for spare change. That is how the German employee sees you. So, next time you come home after one of these situations, fuming at the shop worker, or whoever it may have been, and you're pissed off about them being *rude* or *unfriendly* towards you, keep this notion in your head and everything will become clear as daylight. This is the German way. You're welcome, by the way.

Chapter 2
The Workplace

For those of you who think this book is only going to be about taking the piss out of the Germans and their weird ways, I can assure you (or disappoint you), that once we are past all the initial *finger-pointing,* we shall delve beneath the surface to discover that there are historical, political, social, economic, and even practical reasons for their behaviour. This chapter will examine the mindset of the German population by looking at the workplace, giving the reader a peek under the hood, so to speak.

During my early years in the *Bundesrepublik* (the years 2007 to 2015, to be exact), I was a self-employed musician. I was my own boss, worked at my own speed, with my own goals and aspirations, and basically only ever had to deal with Germans when I needed something from the government or tax office (i.e., almost never). In other words, I was on the periphery of the *real Germany.* I hadn't even scratched the surface; I was just a naïve expat, oblivious to the complexity of the country's social pillars. It was not until I got a proper office job that I finally uncovered the true nature of how the Germans actually tick. The workplace — the place where we as individuals spend most of our time — neatly encapsulates the German mentality.

It's your first day at work:
Bring a cake!

In 2015, I got a job in Berlin, working in the office of a cruise company. I was looking for a change and welcomed the opportunity to take on a new challenge. I moved to Berlin not knowing what the future would have in store for me. Nevertheless, I was looking forward to having a stable job, work colleagues, a monthly paycheck, an office that was not my bedroom, and some sort of a structure in my life. Since the job was still in the music industry, I considered it the right stepping stone in my career development, and, at the *not-so-tender* age of thirty-three, I thought the time was right to get a 'proper job'.

When I first started in my position as a music manager, I was keen to impress everyone with my skill set and my work ethic. I was doing everything I could, helping everyone who asked, and even those who did not. I was a do-gooder, eager to make friends and show everyone how good I was at my job. Obviously, I was young and naïve, thinking that hard work and talent would show my bosses my value, and then, more responsibility would follow; more money, extra recognition and a promotion were just around the corner. In other words, I did not have a blinking clue of how things really work in a mid- to large-scale company in Germany. I was about to learn a very tough lesson.

I remember my first day as if it were yesterday. As

instructed, I arrived at my new workplace at 9:30 sharp. It was a midsize office in the centre of Berlin, close to Checkpoint Charlie. The tall, modern building gave a good first impression, and I was looking forward to the rest of the day. The whole morning I was paraded through the various departments, putting on my best smile and saying hello to everyone, listening attentively to everything anyone had to say, and telling everyone how much I was looking forward to working with them. After the initial orientation was complete, I went to my new office, which was home to three people, myself included. I then decided to pop to the kitchen to see what the coffee situation was like. As I was making myself a brew, a big man in his late thirties, wearing bold glasses, dark khaki commando trousers and a grey T-shirt (which looked as if he'd slept in it for the past week) came through the door. Without stereotyping, I could say with 99 percent certainty that he worked in the tech department. He glanced at me, and then quickly scanned the kitchen, obviously looking for something. Then, half disappointed, he said, "Oh, you're the new guy?" Before I could engage him in a conversation, he added, "And where's the cake?" *Epic fail!*

Different countries, different customs. In Germany, if you are celebrating something, be it your birthday, the birth of your child, or even your first day at work, it is customary that you bring a cake to celebrate. Especially at work, this is an opportunity you don't want to miss. You want to make a good impression. By bringing an offering to the table, you won't need to worry about breaking the ice. Incidentally, the same rule applies at the pub. People will congratulate you — this is customary, of course — but in contrast to the Anglo-Saxons, the birthday boy or girl is the one who buys a round.

Icebreakers

If, like me, you forget the cake, you'll have to resort to other means to break the ice. And that's not as easy as you might think. Having lived in the UK for the best part of my student years, I had become accustomed to Britishness; the polite, easy-on-the-ear banter, the how-are-yous and the customary icebreakers about the weather. These small but essential gestures subliminally say to the other person, "Hey, I understand you, I know how to talk to you, and I respect your customs." Nothing more and nothing less. When I first arrived in Germany, these customs from my former country naturally kicked in and tried to impose themselves — and received a nasty shock. The difference in German mentality became apparent, the moment I first tried to start up a conversation with a stranger.

I vividly remember the first time I stepped into an elevator with other people, as if it were yesterday. It went something like this:

Them: Hello.

Me: Hello, how are you?

Them (*slightly confused by my question*): Why? Do I not look healthy?

And that pretty much killed the natural progression of that conversation. The remainder of the elevator journey was filled with awkward quasi explanations, half-smiles in both directions and what seemed like an excruciatingly long time for the elevator to reach the third floor.

I later learnt that the only thing required of somebody is to say "*Guten Tag!*" when entering the elevator and "*Tschüss*" upon exiting. My internal CPU was imploding. "Why would you want to say 'Hello' and not follow it up with anything else," I wondered. And even more absurdly, "Why the compulsion to say 'Goodbye' to somebody when no conversation has taken place?" Wouldn't it be better to just not say anything at all? It's like playing a Beethoven Sonata without the middle part, merely starting with the exposition and proceeding on to the recap (forgive my musical metaphor — I am a musician, after all). A simpler metaphor would be that it's like getting on the bus, paying the fee and then immediately getting off without travelling. (Although that one is perhaps a bit too extreme).

Whichever way you put it, the shock to the system was at first immense. If you think that the elevator setting is absurd enough, then apply the same principle to waiting rooms. This setting is far more absurd due to the extended amount of time you spend there. Imagine coming in, saying "Hello" to whoever might be sitting there, sitting in silence for anything between twenty and forty minutes, and then getting up and saying "Goodbye". For a very long time, I tried to understand the way German culture, history and any other factors may have had an influence on this, but to no avail. In the end I just accepted it as 'the way it is' and moved on. It was not until much later that I fully grasped the all-important reasons behind the complete disregard for icebreakers in Germany. In particular, this applies to German business culture. The gist of it goes a bit like this: in Germany it is generally accepted that everything and everyone has a purpose to it. Thus, the guy who delivers your post has a job to do, and whether or not he or she likes their job — or you, for that matter — he or she will do it to the letter of the law. It doesn't matter if you are pleasant to them, or if you shout abuse at them. You will still get your package. In other words, you as the customer play no part in the equation that influences the delivery person's decision-making. He or she will not put your package first or last on the delivery route depending on whether or not you've given him or her milk and cookies. And thus, creating any kind of a connection or a rapport with the other person is — de facto — a complete waste of your time. This example can be applied to all spheres of everyday life in Germany and is a cornerstone of the way people interact with each other, as we shall see later on in this book.

Before I get angry shakes of the head in disapproval, I would like to backtrack a bit and say that Germany is not completely devoid of any small talk. It does exist, however the topics used differ greatly from the ones known in the Anglo-Saxon world. For example, after short greetings like *"Naaa"* (Well?), *"Alles fit?"* (All good?) and *"Was geht ab?"* (What's up?), the conversation often steers in a direction which is safe or common to both persons engaging in it. This is bound by the universal law of interaction and applies — well — universally. In the UK, we might talk about the weather, football or — if you're feeling particularly adventurous — politics. In Germany, the most common topics are health, insurance and taxes, and we cover all of these in this book.

So, in the interest of smooth social interactions, here is my guide to icebreakers, German style.

In many cultures the words "How are you" are seen

as an icebreaker; a half-hearted attempt to be polite, or strike up a conversation. However, in Germany, they are treated more literally. Indeed, they suggest that somebody is genuinely interested in your health. So, if you do ask someone, *"Wie geht es Ihnen?"*, be prepared for a lengthy conversation about their health, their various ailments, and the trips to the doctor they've recently made.

Over the years, I have learnt the different approaches one must take in different situations, in order to ensure a smooth progression of the conversation, and to avoid a situation in which you appear strange to the other person. If you live in the North, or in particular in the Hanseatic city of Hamburg, it is common to greet people with a *"Moin"* followed up with a *"Naaa"*, dialling the pitch of the vowel towards the upper frequencies as you pronounce it. An alternative would be to say *"Alles klar?"*, which translates as "All good?" These alternatives are much more culturally acceptable ways of greeting someone than the literal "How are you?". However, they are all informal and thus should only be used with people you already know who are not considerably older than yourself. In other words, the German language has many pitfalls for the unassuming foreigner, and getting to grips with these could take some time. If in doubt, play the monkey card and just repeat what the other person is saying: *"Moin." "Moin." "Naaaa?" "Naaaa?" "Alles klar?" "Alles klar."*

German language is very important to the Germans,

Denglish

and this topic is the subject of a separate chapter later on in this book. In the meantime, I wanted to delve into the use of the English language at work. For somebody like myself — a native English speaker and a translator — this topic is particularly difficult to write about, as it invokes lots of painful memories which I can only describe in terms of a lifecycle, similar to the grief cycle that begins with shock and denial, moves through pain, anger and despair, and eventually transcends into numbness, indifference and acceptance. Having gone through the whole cycle when it comes to *Denglish*, I can finally write this without experiencing painful emotions.

The dictionary defines *Denglisch* as 'a variety of German containing a high proportion of English words'. There are several different types of *Denglish* usage in the German language. For example, there is the straightforward use of English slogans in advertising, such as the German airline Lufthansa's tagline, "There is no better way to fly". Another form of *Denglish* is the dropping of random English words into German sentences. The third one is the gradual creeping of English spelling and grammar into the German syntax, e.g. *'Karl's Friseur'*. Perhaps the most annoying of all, particularly to native English speakers, is the coining of 'English' words that either mean something completely different in the English language, or altogether do not exist. For example, *der Dressman* (male model), *der Smoking* (tuxedo) and *der Moderator* (talk show host). That last one I have a particular problem with, mainly due to the fact that I used to work in a theatre company, where I would constantly hear people say "the moderator" when they referred to the presenter on stage. At first I was adamant to correct everyone who made that mistake, but I eventually gave up, as it turned out to be impossible to *beat the system*. But hearing people say it every day and being powerless to stop them gave me a nervous tick. I still have it. I think if ever there were a trigger that would induce me to embark on a mass shooting spree, that would probably be it.

The other use of English which is very common in Germany is the attempt to incorporate English words into German grammar. For example, downloaden (to download), as in *"Ich habe den File downgeloadet"*. Or *canceln* (to cancel), as in, *"Das Meeting wurde gecancelt"*, pronounced *[gekenzelt]*.

This is not to say, however, that the English language has never borrowed or coined words of its own accord. There has always been a certain amount of "cross-pollination" between the world's languages. Historically, both English and German borrowed heavily from Greek, Latin, French and other languages. English has German loan words such as *angst, gemütlich, kindergarten, masochism, and schadenfreude,* but, in contrast to most Denglish-isms, these are used because there is no true English equivalent. In total contrast, the majority of English terms used in the German language actually replace perfectly good German words; their sole purpose is to make sentences sound *cooler*. Anglo-American influence on the German language can be traced to the business and technology sector, where it can be seen to be doing the most *damage* to the German language. Dramatic proof of this tendency can be seen in the popularity of Bastian Sick's 2004 humorous book entitled *"Der Dativ ist dem Genitiv sein Tod"* (The Dative [Case] Will be the Death of the Genitive). The bestseller (another English word used that is used in Germany) points out the deterioration of the German language *(Sprachverfall)*, caused in part by bad English influences. In all fairness, there is a very practical reason for using English words in place of their German equivalents — they are often shorter and have a much nicer ring to them. For example, let's say one of your colleagues had a brainfart and did something really bad, like posting some dubious political views on the company's Facebook page. There is a flurry of comments and the PR department is up in arms. You could use a German term to describe the action — Empörungswelle (a wave of anger), as in *"Er hat eine Empörungswelle ausgelöst"* (He caused a wave of anger), but the noun in question has no 'bite' to it. The solution: use the English equivalent — 'shitstorm', and add a superlative before it. The result: *'Er hat ein Mega Shitstorm ausgelöst!'* (He caused a massive shitstorm!). Now that's going to turn people's heads, for sure.

On a humorous note, I have seen plenty of examples in German advertising where an attempt to combine both English and German together has gone horribly wrong. Some of the best ones I can remember: *'Kamm inside'* - an unnamed hairdresser's failed attempt to craft a pun from the German word for a comb *(Kamm),* and the English 'come in'. Another hairdressers' fail: *'Funny cuts'.* Whichever way you turn this, I still cannot find a logical explanation. Another favourite of mine was an advertising slogan by a state-sponsored agency, which read, 'Don't drug and drive' — a frankly idiotic attempt at mimicking the 'Don't drink and drive' slogan. The advertising executives presumably didn't realise that the English term needs the addition of the helping verb, 'do'. Or perhaps 'Don't do drugs and drive' didn't sound quite as *in*. And if that's not enough for you, how about going on a 'C-Date', a dating app that apparently promises to find attractive people in your vicinity. For the sake of writing about it, I actually went on the website to see what the 'c' stands for, and turns out it's 'casual'. Interesting slogan, I thought, and, yet, that's not what I thought of initially. My brain was steering towards a quality thing, like the one you get at supermarkets. Do you want the expensive 'Class A' oranges from sunny Spain – the ones that are a perfect size, firm, individually polished, grown without pesticides, and have an invigoratingly fresh citrus aroma? Or the 'Class B' ones that didn't quite fit the high standard of the top supermarkets? Or, if you can't afford those either, you'd have to settle for the scabby ones from Romania; the ones you find in cheap supermarkets with flies hovering around them — the 'Class C'. For me, personally, this was another case of getting it wrong when it comes to attempts to mix German logic with the English language. Then again, perhaps this was precisely the message the company wanted to convey, and, judging from the reviews, they seem to have succeeded.

Another thing to make a vein pop out on your forehead: it is quite common to hear Germans use the *F* word in a conversation, especially when they are conversing in English. This is used either as an exclamation like, "What the f*ck", or to add emphasis: "That is f*cking disgusting." To a native English speaker, such profanity generally has no place in public, except perhaps at a football stadium or a pub, but in Germany the fact that it's a *foreign word* softens the meaning quite considerably. Thus, using it in a work context seems perfectly acceptable. I've even seen that exact expression displayed proudly on the wall of the Arts and Crafts corridor at a high school. I'll let the reader consider that for a moment in silence.

Glossary of most annoying Denglish words:

das Meeting — the meeting
gecancelled — cancelled (verb, past tense)
*What the f*ck* — self explanatory, often used as an exclamation, e.g., "Und ich dachte, what the f*ck!"
brainstormen — to brainstorm
der Shitstorm — a torrent of negative reaction resulting from a comment or action
managen — to manage
downloaden — to download
die Moderation — what presenters say on stage
I've lost count of the amount of times I've hit a brick

Rules rule the rules

wall, unable to get things done due to some stupid technicality in the rule book. And I have to say — Germans are very clear about their rules. There is no such thing as *unwritten rules*. This is because all the rules, down to the most trivial, minute detail, are always written down somewhere, and it's very important that you know where that is. The written rules are the most important factor that governs a workplace, be it an office, a cruise ship or even a spaceship. A novice mistake is to try to bypass — or worse, completely ignore — the rules, thinking that 'as long as you get the same result, the rules can be bent, worked around, or discarded'. If you do make that mistake, you might as well write your own obituary right there and then, because very soon you'll find yourself in a similar situation to Neo in *The Matrix*, fighting a torrent of trained agents from all sides. To put it simply, just read the bloody rulebook. Hang a copy above your desk. Consult it often.

Equally, the Germans are not very good at 'cutting corners', or 'reading between the lines'. Those concepts are as alien to them as the idea of Theresa May (the former British prime minister) putting on heels and a miniskirt, or Boris Johnson getting his hair dyed black. (If you don't get this reference, let's just say that both instances are as rare as finding a polar bear in Africa. And finally, you can never win an argument by pitting common sense against *The Rules,* not in Germany. Sometimes, or in fact, in a lot of situations, the rules prevent you from doing your job efficiently. Then again, efficiency, as I discovered to my dismay, is not rewarded in the German system. This seems like a paradox, particularly considering the fact that 'made in Germany' is a euphemism for all things 'highly efficient', 'process-based', 'super- optimised' and reliable. But when you actually live and work there, you gradually come to see that Germany doesn't quite live up to this description.

Nobody told me

For one thing, Germans love making excuses. Since making mistakes and admitting your own faults and shortcomings is an absolute no-go, Germans are exceptional masters at shifting the blame. It's a trait I was always taught to despise. My own upbringing was the complete opposite, with phrases like 'own up to your mistakes' and 'stop making excuses' drilled into me from a young age. And thus, getting to grips with a nation that has a deep-rooted tradition of excuse-making is that bit more difficult. The most common excuses range from phrases like "I was off sick", "I didn't get the message" and "I was on holiday" to perhaps the most idiotic excuse you'll ever encounter: *"Das wurde mir nicht gesagt"* (Nobody told me). It sounds ridiculous, I know, but to Germans that is a legitimate excuse. To anyone who isn't German, saying something like that would immediately arouse suspicion of your being inept; or, to put it bluntly, it is akin to admitting that you're an imbecile. It's exposing yourself as a lazy dimwit who cannot think for him- or herself; a brainless paper-pusher, one who can never do anything on their own, and has to be told everything like a five-year-old. And yet, evidently, Germans have no problem in doing just that, because they will happily use this excuse at every possible opportunity.

Didn't you get the memo?

Another thing holding back efficiency is Germany's penchant for emails. Back when I was an employee at the cruise ship company, I was inundated by emails every day. At that time I pretty much ignored anything that didn't explicitly mention my name, and I cared very little about bureaucracy and company politics. More recently, having taken my career in a different direction to become a teacher at a German school, I can't help but give my younger self a sarcastic smirk; the kind of reaction that older and more experienced people have when they want to say: "Ah, little did you know, my young Skywalker, just you wait." In other words, if your employer is the German state (as mine now is), the amount of paperwork you do quadruples. Thus you can expect anything between thirty and fifty emails clogging up your inbox every single day. These range from official reports from the Department of Education, which are usually forwarded on by the principal, to reports by class teachers, heads of various years, various task groups, parent groups, and a plethora of meeting protocols. Every email tends to contain pages upon pages of information — written using pompous official wording — most of which has absolutely nothing to do with your day-to-day tasks.

At first, I would go through pages and pages of font-size-eleven emails, feeling completely useless, skimming through official reports and other general stuff that had absolutely no meaning to me. I had passed the hardest possible test in German — C2 level — the mother of all language tests. I felt like I had finally mastered the language and won the battle against my demons in the closet (Frau Schumacher, my German teacher at the university, being one of them). And yet, there I was, trying to grasp the meaning of sentences upon sentences comprising compound nouns that were completely and utterly incomprehensible. At that point I seriously considered jacking it all in, and going back to my happy-go-lucky life as a musician. After weeks of sleepless nights spent reading, crying and Google translating, I finally managed to work out how to differentiate between the information that actually had any relevance, and the stuff that should just go straight in the trash.

I noticed that, when dealing with Germans, there is no such thing as a short email. Even a short response would be at least a paragraph. The real test comes when — in a conversation — somebody refers to an email sent three months ago and expects you to know what the heck they're talking about. I wish that were a joke, but it's not. People really do expect you to keep track of *all* email communication dating back as far as three months, and are likely to test you by referring to one such email with an exact date and time sent. As an example, I've had numerous conversations that went something like this:

Mr X: Mr. Gaziri, I remind you of the email sent 6th July at 11:55, in which it was explicitly stated that the deadline is 16th November.
Me: Ehm, you mean an email four months ago, when the initial 12-page briefing was sent?
Mr X: Yes, exactly that!
Me: Well, gee, I thought the world was going to end at some point over the last four months, so I just deleted your stupid 12-page, font-size-11 mail, you stupid tw*t.

Of course, despite my rebellious nature, I wouldn't dream of ever replying in such a way, and, however preposterous it may seem to non-Germans, you will be expected to keep up with these kinds of communications, in the same way one would expect you to turn up to work wearing pants. To add insult to injury, there is no such thing as a *friendly reminder* — the emails people send to make sure you haven't forgotten about a deadline, reminders that take into account the fact that people have a million other things going through their heads every day and that keeping up with all of these things is, to say the least, a bit difficult. Alas, it doesn't work like that in Germany. Here, you are expected to make a note of all the important appointments in your calendar, set reminders as needed, and generally plan everything you do months in advance. Perhaps this is not that different to the rest of the modern technological world, you might retort. In a way, yes — but one point where Germany differs from other countries is that asking or double-checking is a sign of incompetence and is treated in a negative way. Double-checking with colleagues has always made me feel like I'm being dismissed as incompetent. Your colleagues will most likely think that you're not on top of things. It's a waste of time anyway, since the most likely outcome is that, instead of telling you what you need to know, they will refer you to the original email sent on the fifth of never!

The CC syndrome

Have you ever found yourself spending ages reading emails from your colleagues about useless details that they could clarify in an instant by going directly to the source? They could, but instead they prefer to send out a mass email with half of the company in the CC. You don't personally have any direct connection to what they're emailing about, but just to show you're 'actively involved in the subject' you force yourself to click 'reply all' and write a one-liner, thereby contributing to the volume of email garbage spreading through the ether; the collective vomit that everyone spits out and passes around. Does this sound familiar to you? Here's another one: Have you ever replied to a client with a direct inquiry that you alone solved, but you put your boss in CC, just to show him or her that you're 'dealing' with the issue? And here's the best one of all: Have you ever come into the office extra early or stayed extra late and the minute you got in — or just before you left — sent some useless email to your boss, with the sole purpose of showing the 'clock time' that you're already, or still, at work? If all of this applies to you, then you have a classic case of the 'CC syndrome'.

If you ask anyone working in a managerial position in a mid- to large-scale company about the need for 'CC', they will tell you that it's essential for transparency. And, to a certain degree, I agree that involving everyone in the issue ensures that nobody is left behind, so to speak. On the other hand, this procedure does have the unfortunate effect of compounding the number of times your inbox's incoming message alert goes 'pling', to the power of one hundred. Discussions and arguments break out, and so on and so forth. It becomes akin to a Facebook thread, in which everyone has to have their say. When I worked for the cruise ship company, one of my colleagues always insisted on me sending her everything in an email, even things we had just spoken about in a meeting. This was unfathomable to me, since it seemed that I was just being made to do the same work twice, and thus wasting valuable time on a task that she should have sorted out by herself. It was only after a year or so that I truly understood the reason behind this, and it's a valid one indeed. When something goes 'pear-shaped', or even 'tits up', and the proverbial finger of blame is looking for its victim, the colleague in question could always show a paper trail demonstrating everything she had done, and prove to everyone that she was not at fault, since 'she had done exactly what was requested in the email and followed the task to the letter' — and, one has to add, not an iota more.

Indeed, the whole thinking process in the German workplace boils down to two simple thoughts:

- Ensure you have proof that you have done everything by the book.
- Ensure that the chain of command does not stop with you

Following these simple rules allows you to shift the blame onto someone else, if ever something bad should happen. For example, if your boss comes down hard on you because his or her boss did the same, you can show him or her that a) you did everything to the letter of the law; and b) you have a paper trail to prove it, since all of the emails have your boss in the 'CC', thus taking yourself out of the *Schusslinie* (line of fire). This mentality forms the very cornerstone of any corporate mindset in Germany, and I'll explain why.

Results vs. Process

Working at a German company is very different to working for an English one, or a Scandinavian one, and especially an American company. All of the above-mentioned are *results-driven*, meaning that great emphasis is placed on the simplifying of processes, maximising efficiency, minimising bureaucracy and encouraging good results with a rewards-driven system. Here in Germany, in contrast, the system is process-based, loyalty-driven, overly bureaucratic and highly inefficient. Alas, it is not a system in which skill, competence and speed are rewarded. On the contrary, the model employee seems to generally be incompetent, takes way too long to complete a task, but is 100 percent loyal and so always toes the party line, so to speak. This, of course, doesn't apply to the new wave of start-ups, which are popping up in Berlin at a staggering rate, all led by 20-something bosses keen on incorporating the *Silicon Valley* models. Nor does it apply to small-scale companies that embrace the Anglo-American approach. No, we're talking about a mid- to large-scale German company with 150 plus employees, saturated with hierarchical layers and formal addresses, drowning in overcomplicated processes and self-imposed, rigid structures; one where the CEOs and board of directors are all 50-something, proper old-school, conservative types, resistant to change and with very little clue about the changing business climate (or diversity, for that matter).

If you work with German companies as a contractor, supplier, customer — basically if you have a business relationship with them — and you're going into meetings for whatever reason, it might be helpful to take note of the following dos and don'ts of business meetings in Germany:

- When scheduling a meeting, make sure that your German counterpart has put it in their calendar, and write them an email confirming your attendance. Irrespective of whether you have just got off the phone, or been in a meeting with that person.

- Never turn up at your boss's office without an appointment, or call them without prior notice. Germans hate surprises, and they will despise you for ruining their carefully planned day.

- If you're dealing with a particular person in a company, and for some reason they are away, be it on a holiday, sick leave, or whatever other reason, don't expect anyone to take over and deal with your query. Even if your personal business sense is telling you otherwise, this is not the German way.

- Don't start your presentation with a joke. In fact, forget the jokes altogether. They are not socially acceptable at work and guaranteed to cause awkward silence, sweat on the back of your neck, confused looks, and more awkwardness, especially if you try to explain them to your audience.

- The Germans have a habit of explaining everything twice, thrice, or even four times, without stopping once to check if it's necessary. It is very easy to think that you're being treated like a child or somebody with a very low IQ, but you'll have to resist the urge to interrupt. Instead, wait patiently until they have finished, and, as clearly as you possibly can: a) tell the person you have understood; b) regurgitate the information that they have just given you; and c) tell them your plan of action, which must also include the reasons behind your decisions, alternatives and contingency plans. There's also a bonus point up for grabs if you carry out d), which is concluding by saying that you'll send them an email summarising everything that was discussed.

- Without that last point, your meeting will be rendered ineffective, useless, de facto — void, and will cause you a lot of agro, so make sure you send them that f*cking email.

Employment laws

If you think that I'm completely bonkers by suggesting that all employees in Germany ever think about is ensuring their own safety and survival in case of something going pear-shaped, then let's put this whole thing into context.

German citizens enjoy some of the best employment conditions in Europe, and subsequently on the planet. For example, if you have just started a new job at company XYZ, you will have an initial trial period — the so-called Probezeit — which lasts for six months. After that, your contract becomes permanent for all eternity and it is almost impossible for an employer to fire you, so long as you play by the rules. Aside from that, there are only two scenarios in which you can lose your job: the first one is if the company has to restructure and your job no longer exists. In this case you will be made redundant. In Germany the standard phrase for that is *'aus betrieblichen Gründen'* (due to operational circumstances). In such a case, the employee will get severance pay, which is calculated based on the number of years they have worked for that company, and their salary. The minimum payoff is usually around three months' salary. The other scenario in which you might be made unemployed is if the company goes belly-up and files for insolvency. In such a case, you may be put on furlough (known as *'Kurzarbeit'* in Germany) and you might eventually lose your job. The latter scenario is something a lot of people experienced during the COVID-19 pandemic. But if you do find yourself out of work in the German system, there are always plenty of options for you to get back on your horse. Fancy working in a kebab shop?

Döner Fachkraft Ausbildung

For years, I was unable to understand why people in Germany are so allergic to being multi-skilled. In workplaces the job titles are as precise as you could possibly imagine. Doing anything outside of your job description is frowned upon, and in some cases even amounts to a punishable offence. The whole German economy is based upon this principle, which is partly why they can boast a very low unemployment rate. In fact, I would dare to go even further and state that the whole educational system is based around this principle too. Hence why a lot of people do apprenticeships, which are specifically tailored for specific jobs. And I'm not talking about doing an apprenticeship to be a mechanic or a plumber. We're talking about jobs in the banking and insurance sectors too. If you want to start working as a *'Bank Angestellter'* (bank employee) in Germany, you'd need to do a training course which is conveniently tittled *Studium zum Bank Angestellter* (study for a bank employee). If you wanted to get into insurance, equally you'd need to study a course to become a *Versicherungsmakler* (insurance broker). Anyone fickle enough to think that a general degree could also land them a job in a different industry will soon discover they have a mountain to climb, to put it mildly. This is one of the reasons why the Germans are so obsessed with their *Curriculum Vitae*, their official reference letters from previous employers, called a *Zeugnis*, and their job titles.

The word *Ausbildung* — essentially meaning *training* — is a mantra when it comes to anything job-related in Germany. As I've already explained, the *Bundesrepublik* is all about qualifications. If you want to get a job in any field, irrespective of the skills required, you will need to get a job-specific qualification. This, as you might expect, is taken quite literally in Germany: even low-skilled jobs like cashiers, waiters or even donner meat sellers require the applicant to have exactly the right kind of qualifications. Anybody reading this might find it absurd —a two-year Ausbildung in order to sell kebabs in a kebab shop or work as a waiter, surely not! — But that's how it is. Thus, if you want to work as a salesperson in a hotel, you would need to train as a *Hotelkaufmann or Hotelkauffrau,* which is the career path for a sales person in a hotel. If you then wanted to switch to selling pork pies, or pencils, you would need to do an additional training programme, specifically titled *pork-pie-sales-person,* or *office-sup-plies-sales-person,* in order to change careers. For each training programme you complete, you get a certificate which states something along the lines of: "*This certifies that John Smith has successfully completed a two-year course as a meat packer in accordance with the German meat packing standards.*" Hurray! Whoopty do!

For a long time I couldn't comprehend how such an absurd system could be allowed to continue, but after learning more about German employment laws, lots of things began to fall into place. Firstly, as a general rule, an *Ausbildung* is heavily subsidised by the government. So if a company takes on trainees, a great chunk of their wages will be paid for by public funds, rather than out of the company's budget. There are also plenty of tandem programmes between institutions and companies that allow students to do part of their training — the so-called 'placement' — in a company. These, too, are heavily subsidised by the government. And, thirdly, it's *protocol*. We have already learned that insurance is one of the cornerstones of life in the *Bundesrepublik*, as it governs almost every stage and aspect of people's lives. It should therefore come as no surprise that companies in Germany are required to follow strict guidelines in all of their business practices. A meat packer must be a *qualified meat packer;* this will be a prerequisite on the part of the insurer, in case something goes south — for instance if an unhappy customer decides to sue because his donner meat was served by somebody who was unqualified to serve donner meat, or some safety standard was not adhered to. Thus, a company will only be able to hire people who have the required certificate.

Job titles

Germany can definitely be added to the list of countries where job titles are taken very seriously, almost as a kind of status. You will probably experience this at some point in your professional career. For example, you might refer to somebody as a 'manager', and find yourself immediately corrected when the person tells you they are in fact a 'senior manager'. Or perhaps you happen to call someone a 'senior manager', when in fact you are facing a 'department head', and so on and so forth. This to me is a strange concept, particularly in comparison to the UK, where at the beginning of the new millenium job titles were simply plucked from thin air. Making everything more 'marketable' was the zeitgeist of the noughties, giving people more importance and a sense of empowerment (whatever that may be), whilst at the same time making everything sound more 'sassy' and 'sexy'. Effectively, this meant that every office worker became an 'office manager'; waiters and waitresses became 'service staff'; stewards and stewardesses became 'flight attendants', and even your local bin man became an 'area facility manager' — just like that, overnight. Thus, you can imagine that, when I realised how much importance was given to job titles in the *Bundesrepublik*, it did make me chuckle a bit — but only at first. Very soon, once the hard reality set in, my smirk swiftly disappeared.

So what is the big deal with job titles in Germany, you may ask? Alas, there is no one short answer to this. Essentially, it boils down to the career ladder and the way salaries are structured. In a stark contrast to many other countries, there is a high degree of transparency in how much each professional gets paid. You can test this yourself by googling the salaries of different professions and see the results within seconds. You'll be surprised to find detailed information on pretty much any job title, from a *Bankangestellter* to a mid-tier manager in a media consultancy; a partner in a law firm, or even a courtroom judge. It's all there, open to the public. When it comes to job titles, other factors play a role as well as the salary. For example, a senior manager must have a certain number of years' experience, and will have jumped through quite a few hoops in order to get to that position. In contrast, a junior manager is somebody who has just started out in their profession. At the very bottom of the ladder, you'll find interns, apprentices, and the so-called 450-euro-per-month contractors.

Here are a few job titles that you can find in most industries, with an explanation of what they actually mean:

Azubi (apprentice): You're on an official training programme, which is heavily subsidised by the state.

Praktikant (intern): You do all the work that paid managers do, but without getting paid.

Junior Manager: As a young professional with little or no industry experience, this is your first proper job, with a real salary. You can finally move out of your parents' place.

Manager: You've reached mid-management level and can now give all the crap tasks to the interns and junior managers, whilst you dedicate more valuable time to sucking up to the big bosses. You can finally afford to get out of shared accommodation and rent your own place.

Senior Manager: A few more years down the line, and you've reached a level where you can book your own business trips without having to ask for permission. You can leave all the job-related tasks to the managers and concentrate solely on your next promotion and company politics.

Head of Department: You've finally made it. After all those years of petty squabbles, inter-departmental budgeting feuds, sucking up to the bosses and gambling on the 'winning horse', you have finally reached the top echelon. Unfortunately for you, this comes with the realisation that you've hit the ceiling. Getting higher up is only possible if one of the top bosses drops dead or leaves for another job, somewhere higher up the food chain. You've now got a choice: concentrate on your gardening and other hobbies, or seek a career change.

Director: Your days are constantly filled with averting attacks on your budget by other directors, and 'keeping a lid' on a multitude of disasters before they manage to find their way out into the open. You secretly long for the time when you were a junior manager, when things were so simple and straightforward.

At this point, the reader might rightly exclaim, "But this is how it works in every country! What's so different about Germany?" Well, job titles may appear to be exactly the same on the surface, but there is one big difference: in this country, much more weight is given to job titles, no matter which industry you're in. People cling to them as though their livelihoods depended on it. Constant internal power squabbles, as well as lots of legislative red tape — like the constant attempts to increase budgets and the number of staff allocated to each department — play a key role in this too. Oftentimes, it is as much about measuring who's got the bigger *Schtick*, as much anything else. Naturally there are exceptions, even in Germany, and if you look at all the startups and new tech companies, whose aim is to deliberately disrupt this somewhat outdated system, you'll definitely notice a reverse of that trend. Hence why Google might have a job title like 'Minister of Fun'. But apart from that exception, the majority fall under the umbrella of the status quo, as described above, and you'll see people obsessing over their job titles and job descriptions. Which brings me to the next point — the CV. The German word for that is *Lebenslauf*, and you'll find that everyone is equally obsessed with it — individuals and hiring managers alike. So what's the big deal?

German CVs

If you're new to the German job market, and you're actively looking for employment, then I would seriously advise you to get a professional CV writer to help you out. This will save you a lot of time learning about this German peculiarity from scratch — which is no picnic, I can assure you. I found this out the hard way, back in the days when I was naïve, thinking that highlighting my extensive experience in many different fields, coupled with having a 'personality' and 'standing out', would put me a step ahead of the other applicants. I couldn't have been more wrong. In order to save you some blushes in front of your prospective employers, I've compiled a list of things that should give you a nudge in the right direction when it comes to German CVs, or, at least help you avoid the big mistakes I made when applying for jobs.

- **Follow the rules:** Forget trying to bring out your personality; this is frowned upon in this country. Instead, concentrate on the general format the Germans use for their CVs. Make sure you follow it to the letter.

- **Keep it specific:** Your CV should be written like a personal data sheet (yes, it's as exciting as it sounds), listing every task you did in your previous job, down to the most boring one. This should be done in bullet-point format.
- **Keep it relevant:** Do not bring in your work experience from other industries, unless relevant to the job, or specifically asked for in the job description. This is viewed the same way as having gaps in your CV; jumping between different industry sectors will only put you at a disadvantage.
- **Include a photo:** Your photo should always be serious and 'boring'. You can put on an 'inner smile', but showing your teeth is a no-no.
- **Mind the gap:** Having a gap in your CV is akin to having the word 'prison' written on it. At least, that's how it's viewed here.
- **List your hobbies:** Put two or three hobbies at the end. Less than that will make it sound like you're a hermit, and more than three could be misconstrued as you preferring your hobbies to the actual work (not a thing you want to admit, at least not officially).
- **The language:** Your CV must be in German, for obvious reasons.
- **Leave the personality out:** You do not need to write a paragraph about your personality and boast how 'dedicated' or 'flexible' you are. There is time and place for that — namely, in your motivational letter (*Bewerbungsschreiben*).

Knowing how to present your best side to potential employers in Germany is one thing. Being able to decode the job advert to decide if the role suits your qualifications and career aspirations is another. Having worked in all corners of the media industry, I would like to share my experience of how to interpret certain word choices in job descriptions and what they actually mean — albeit with a bit of exaggeration. Here's my read-between-the-lines guide to German job descriptions:

- **Flexible:** Be prepared to work long hours and weekends.
- **Highly motivated:** Your pay is going to be sh*te, so you'll need to have other motivational factors for getting out of bed.
- **Team player:** You will need to be loyal and follow rules and regulations set by the company without questioning them.
- **Hands-on approach:** You'll have to do lots of other tasks that are not part of your job description.
- **Young professional:** You've just come out of university, and have absolutely no blinking clue — about anything.
- **Flat organisational structure:** Our company bosses are following in the footsteps of startup companies, wanting to appear fresh, cool and empowering. The smallish size of the company allows that — for now — but the bosses still get to call the shots as they see fit.

Your first written warning:
The Abmahnung

Reading the word aloud in three distinct syllables, the reader could be forgiven for assuming it was borrowed from Mandarin, or Cantonese, but I can assure you this is indeed German. As I already mentioned, it is very difficult to get fired in Germany. The laws are all in favour of the employee, and as such, if your boss decides to get rid of you, he or she will have to follow strict guidelines in order to do so. The first step is the so-called *Ab–mah–nung* — a written warning, which is issued if you've committed a serious offence. And I'm not talking about trivial stuff like writing 'big douche' on your boss's office door, or handing in a project past its deadline. It has to be something you did that directly contradicted the written obligations as stated in your written contract or agreement. A classic case would be time-keeping, or missing meetings without a valid excuse (such as going to the doctor — which we will come to in just a moment). If you get a written warning, it means that next time you screw up, you can be catapulted straight out of the front door with all your belongings, and, without an obligation to give you the three months' (paid) notice (*Kündigung* in German). There are two main types of notices you can get: a *Betriebsbedingte Kündigung,* which is a way of saying that you've been made redundant or quit your job under normal circumstances. The other one is called an *Außerordentliche Kündigung* (basically getting the sack). If you are worried about getting the boot, as most Germans are — pretty much all the time — you can get yourself a *Rechtsschutzversicherung* (legal insurance). Just make sure you tick the box which says 'workplace' when filling out the form. In the next chapter we'll talk about what happens when you're unemployed.

Unemployment benefits

Being unemployed in Germany can sometimes mean doing more work than when you were actually working. It's an oxymoron. You might think that you're 'free again', and you can finally book that backpacking holiday to Asia, or start that DIY project you've been putting off for years. Alas, it is not that simple – not in Germany.

Let me explain. On the one hand, Germany is a country that is governed by bureaucracy and lots and lots of paperwork. The minute you become unemployed, you are required by law to register with the unemployment agency – *die Agentur für Arbeit,* also known as the Arbeitsamt. A few days after you register, you can expect to receive a very large envelope through the post. Once you open it, you'll be thrown in at the deep end – a dark, gloomy, bottomless pit, the likes of which you've never seen before. I'm sorry if this sounds ominous, but, in fact, it kind of is. In that envelope, you'll find a huge wad of paper with different forms to fill out, along with a wad of pages known as the *Merkblatt für Arbeitslose,* a handout explaining your *Rechte und Pflichten* — your rights and obligations. This might sound quite normal to you, and — in a way — it is. However, there are some fundamental differences which you need to acquaint yourself with. Before you even qualify for the benefit, you need to wade through pages upon pages of highly technical terminology, with equally difficult explanations written in font size ten. To understand what's going on, you will most likely need a degree in German (un)employment law, and I wish I was joking. There's no use phoning the call centre and asking them stupid questions, because they will talk to you using the same terminology, the same long and complicated sentences, and it will get you absolutely nowhere. Even checking out online forums will not be very helpful, as you will face similar problems there too. You will have to quietly acknowledge that you are alone in the universe, and your only friend is Google Translate (unless your spouse is German and can digest the whole thing for you, in which case — as they say — ignorance is bliss, and you can bravely ignore this whole section and move on). But assuming you're not so lucky, you'll need to start at the very bottom of the unemployment pit by learning the terminology. Don't get disheartened, but it will take weeks, if not months, to fully understand how the unemployment process works in Germany. I counted the number of *Fachwörter* (technical terms) used in the booklet, and I lost count at 202. I'm talking long compound nouns like *Bemessungsgrundlage*, or endless words that begin with the noun Arbeit-, followed by a different compound noun. This, along with all the legal jargon, will drive you close to insanity. To give you a headstart, below I've listed some things that I had to find out the hard way.

Merkblatt für Arbeitslose 1. This is a 102-page handout which will be sent to you (the big wad of paper I mentioned). This will be your bible for the duration of your unemployment. Study it every day, pray with it, do whatever is necessary to understand every single word that is written in there.

ALG-1 & ALG-2: The benefit you initially receive is called Arbeitslosengeld 1 (often abbreviated to ALG-1). This is different to ALG-2, also known as Hartz-IV, which is designed for people who are out of work for more than eighteen months, those whose living circumstances are below the minimum subsistence threshold, and those who are unable to pay basic rent and living costs themselves.

"Actively looking for work": Once you get accepted as a job seeker — Arbeitssuchende — you have to actively look for work. This means signing up on their website, attending every interview or seminar they assign you to, re-writing your resume, and doing whatever it takes, in the eyes of the German state, to get a job as soon as possible.

Document threats: Note that every letter from the Arbeitsamt will contain a sentence at the end which will basically sound like a threat — and it generally is. It goes something like this: "You are required by law to submit this by [...]. Failure to do so may give us grounds to withhold your benefits, or cancel them altogether." This threat is part of the German DNA. Living under the constant threat of consequences and reprimands is what makes them tick. Without any doubt, you will despise these end of the document threats, but there is absolutely nothing you can do about them. Just stay calm, take a deep breath, and carry on.

Leaving the city: If you leave your home city, for whatever reason, you will lose your benefit for that period of time. Additionally, you have to inform the Arbeitsamt by law about your going away.

Holiday days: It sounds crazy, but even as an unemployed person, you are allowed to take holiday days (let's face it, you need a break from writing all of those job applications). You get approximately the same number of days as if you were in employment.

Your unemployment benefit: As a rule of thumb, you get up to 67 percent of your income paid by the Arbeitsamt, for a maximum of eighteen months. The actual amount and duration varies depending on your tax bracket (if you're single or married, and if you have kids), your age, and how long you have been contributing to social security in Germany.

Mini-jobbing and freelancing: You are allowed to take up a so-called 'mini-job' while you are unemployed, or do freelance work, as long as it does not exceed 14.5 hours per week. You'll need to fill out a form for that on a weekly basis. If you pick up temporary work that exceeds 14.5 hours per week, your benefits will be suspended, but will resume once you are back on your job seeker's status.

Expenses: If you get an interview outside of your city, the Arbeitsamt will reimburse you for your trip, provided you travel with standard second class transport.

Residency status: Beware that getting state aid for longer than six months in a two year period will have a negative effect on your residency permit application, i.e. you won't get one.

Relocation: If you have found a job in another city and have to relocate, you can request your local Arbeitsamt to pay for the costs. Not only that, but you can also request for an advance from them to cover renovation costs and a security deposit on your new flat.

"I'm going to the doctor"

And, finally, if ever there were an excuse, a magic pill, a silver bullet for getting out of work; a joker to keep in your pocket, ready to be pulled out when needed, wouldn't that solve all of your problems? Oh, wait, there is! All you have to do is say that you're not feeling well and you have to go to the doctor *cough*, and *hey presto!* There is absolutely nothing any superior can say or do to counter that. It doesn't matter if the workload is massive, if the phone won't stop ringing, if a deadline is looming, or if they know that you're faking it — it simply doesn't matter. Everyone has to follow the same *protocol*, as with everything else in the workplace. It's not the UK, the US, or any other first world country, where, in order to miss work due to sickness, you'd have to have been hit by a truck full of explosives, or had your leg amputated by an oncoming train, or at the very least been kidnapped by ISIS. In fact, in the UK, you could put on the biggest show by coughing up blood, eyes watering, mucus coming out of your nose, crawling along the floor from fever and headache — and the only thing your boss might say is, "Aww, poor you, why don't you go to reception and take a couple of paracetamol and we'll see you back here in five minutes, aw-kay?" But in Germany, sickness is the silver bullet. Remember that. Now that you've acquainted yourself with the workplace, it's time to have a closer look at the German language and culture, which is the subject of next chapter.

Chapter 3
German Language and Culture

There is an old cliché that the worst spies in the world are German. In other words — they are the worst at keeping secrets. Ridiculous, you might say, but if we take a closer look at the German mentality, we might discover an element of truth in this statement. Growing up in the UK, I learnt the most important traits of 'being British'. They are like the ten commandments, and breaking any of them will undoubtedly put you on the wrong foot with the Brits. One of the most important ones is 'do not pry' (basically, 'mind your own business'). Let's say you ask your British friend something really simple like, "What are you up to tonight?" He or she might answer in one of the following ways: "Ah, not much, you?" or "Gotta be somewhere." Both answers are very vague, but somebody who is accustomed to these responses will interpret them in the correct way and make their own conclusions. The first response basically means, "I'm not doing anything, let's hang out." The second response should be interpreted as, "I'm busy". In the first instance, you are subliminally invited to continue the conversation. In the second instance, you are basically prohibited from inquiring further. The person would get very annoyed if you followed up with a line of inquiry on the second response, for instance by saying, "Where have you got to be?" That's a no-no and breaks the sacred commandment, 'Thou shalt not be nosy.' Indeed, being vague and giving as little as information as possible is an important pillar of the British culture, one that should not be underestimated by any means. And, if you wanted to find an antithesis of that culture, you would not need to look far — welcome to

Germany. In this chapter, I'll examine the key elements of the German language and how it is used — both linguistically and culturally speaking — as well as giving some basic dos and don'ts that expats should bear in mind when conversing with German people.

English vs. German: The polar opposites

As a foreigner living in Germany, you will undoubtedly experience a profound sense of cultural shock at first. The time it will take for you to adapt to German culture depends on your own culture and how closely it aligns with the customs of the *Bundesrepublik*. For example, Eastern European and Asian emigres tend to adapt very quickly, whereas those from Hispanic nations and the Arab-speaking world, and particularly the native English speakers, tend to find it more difficult to get used to. I'd like to briefly examine the latter — for obvious reasons.

In my view, the main reason native English speakers find it so hard to adapt lies in some inherently 'English' cultural traits. If you were born and bred in the USA, UK, Australia, or any other Anglo-Saxon territory, you might not have a conscious sense of what these traits are, but any foreigner living in the UK will have had to get used to this *Englishness*, and could therefore give you a pretty decent summary. To define what *Englishness* actually is, and understand it, you could watch Monty Python's *Life of Brian* (1979), or *Little Britain* (2003), or even watch an episode of *Have I Got News for You*. To make it a bit more clear to our non-native-English readers, being English can be summed up in a few quick sentences as follows:

- The Anglo-Saxons are always saying "Sorry" — for everything. It's in their DNA. The last thing you'd want is for somebody to think that you are rude, in any way. So the apology works kind of like a preemptive attack, dispelling the possibility of anyone being offended, for whatever reason.
- The Anglo-Saxons like to show their wit and joke a lot. Humour is not just something the Brits do during dedicated hours. Humour is an essential part of their everyday life.
- The Anglo-Saxons adore self-mockery, self-effacement and being overly humble. Being humble is one of the greatest virtues in British social etiquette. On the contrary, arrogance is possibly the worst. Talking about one's own success would be seen as arrogant, so people tend to play it down instead, showing their humble side, which in retrospect, makes others believe that their achievements are even greater than they are letting on.
- The Anglo-Saxons do not pry. They never ask awkward questions, or put others in an uncomfortable situation — no matter what.
- The Anglo-Saxons are always vague, often using phrases like 'might', 'could', 'play it by ear', and referring to themselves in the third person. They like

to keep their options open, and hate being pinned down, hence why they will often struggle giving you exact time of a meeting, instead resorting to phrases like 'five-ish'.

Unlike the Brits, the Americans, the Scandinavians, the Russians, the Arabs (and those are just the cultures that I have a first-hand experience in — it could well possibly apply to almost every other nation in the world and beyond), the Germans hate the two 'As': ambivalence and ambiguity. There is nothing worse for them than talking to somebody who is being vague, uncertain, unsure, or uses literary or imaginative expressions when explaining something. Imagine answering a direct question about a specific thing with something like, "One could only assume..." This will agitate a German to the point of despair. Best case scenario: He or she will inundate you with follow-up questions, forcing you to explain every minute detail of any part of the sentence that wasn't clear to them. Worst case scenario: They will get very annoyed with you and might even report you to the *'Ordnungsamt'*, which is a type of a street patrol that ensures that nobody is breaking the law.

The fact is that German language is very *literal* and unambiguous. This epitomises the very essence of being German. Indeed, that unequivocal and unambiguous nature is rooted in every German at a very young age. It's in their DNA. Let's use a language example for the sake of argument. A sandwich in German is called a *'sandwich'*, which in German pronunciation sounds more like 'Send-vitch'. But before they adopted this particular Anglicism it was called a *Butterbrot,* literally 'butter bread'. A wardrobe is called a *Kleiderschrank,* which is a combination of the words for 'clothes' and 'drawer'. A pedestrian is called a *Fussgänger* — literally, a foot-walker. Furthermore, the word for refrigerator is taken from two nouns: *kühlen* (to cool) and *Schrank* (cupboard). Put those together and *hey presto*, you've got a *Kühlschrank*, a cool cupboard. A veterinarian in German is called a Tierarzt, literally an 'animal doctor'. And that's the basic principle of all nouns. The trouble starts when the words get longer and longer. You have to navigate through a terrain of compound nouns like *Aufenthaltsgenehmigung*, meaning 'leave to remain'. Anyone from the USA or Canada residing in Germany will be familiar with that term. Another word we can reference here is, coincidentally, the title for the most boring job in Germany — namely, *Sachbearbeiter*. In English the translation would be a *clerk*, but the German compound noun contains the words '*Sache*' (thing) and '*Bearbeiter*' (a person dealing with something). So, basically, if you've got that invigorating job title, you're literally a 'person dealing with things'. Now, if that doesn't get you all excited about your first day at work, then I'm not sure what will. Imagine doing that for the rest of your life. It reminds me of a cult film from the nineties called *Office Space,* and one of its protagonists, Melvin, who is an introvert who gets pushed around by everyone, and eventually ends up working in the basement with no pay, due to some 'company restructuring'. The point is, could you imagine working as a *Sachbearbeiter* for the rest of your life? I'd rather die a painful death and have my remains fed to alligators, but that's just me.

It could be said that the German language itself is about as ambiguous as a brick wall, and this indeed gives us an insight into the mind of its people. Things like 'reading between the lines', an Anglo-Saxon trait of translating the meaning of what is not being said, rather than taking the sentence literally, simply does not exist in the *Bundesrepublik*. There is nothing worse for a German than hearing somebody saying "not sure", or god forbid a metaphor to answer a very clear and precise question like "what are you doing on Friday the 22nd of April between eight and ten pm?"

Over the years, though, I have learnt that not all forms of literary inflation are lost on Germans. Irony, for one, is used amply in everyday conversations. For example, the words *klar* (clear) and *sicher* (sure), are often used as vehicles of irony, in exactly the same way they are used in the English language. The only notable difference, however, is the intonation. When you want to accentuate an ironic response, you would use a prolonged vowel, stretching the word out. The longer you stretch the vowel, the more ironic it will sound. But be careful: you can only do this with certain words. You can't, for example, use the word ja in that same manner. If you did, you would more likely be seen as an idiot. If you wanted to be ironic with the word 'yes', in German you'd have to say it twice in quick succession — *ja ja*. This will get you the ironic effect you're after.

Incidentally, the longest word in the German language consists of no fewer than eighty letters. At least that's what Google says, and I'm quite content with using it as an example here. If anyone finds a longer one, then please feel free to file an official complaint with the Federal Bureau for Linguistics, Cartography and Etymology, provided you can first figure out the compound noun for that. And thus, at **eighty letters,** the longest word ever composed in German is *Donaudampfschifffahrtselektrizitätenhauptbetriebswerkbauunterbeamtengesellschaft,* the "Association for Subordinate Officials of the Head Office Management of the Danube Steamboat Electrical Services". Try saying that out loud.

Learning German as a foreigner

If you're trying to learn German as a beginner, you will often find that people switch to English as soon as they realise that you're a foreigner. My wife, who has just started learning German, thinks it's a nuisance, because she doesn't get the chance to practise enough, and that sentiment is echoed by many foreigners in the same position. I can assure you, however, that once you've reached a certain level of fluency, i.e. you've crossed the magic threshold (otherwise known as B2 on the CEFR scale), even the simplest conversation with a regular German person will land you in a bottomless pit of words, articles, expressions, colloquialisms, dialects, terminology and compound nouns — enough to keep you awake at night for many years to come — and you'll miss the days when your German was bad enough to force people to revert to English to protect their ears. As soon as you cross that threshold, you will be expected to know the correct articles of nouns (more on those in just a second), and all the terminology used in governmental offices, including the tax office and the job centre, at the doctors and, of course, at the *Baumarkt*, as I elaborately explained in Chapter 1.

It is a great incentive that Germany has so many different language schools, both private and state-funded. For example, if you googled 'learn German' in Hamburg right now, you'd get over twenty location pins in the city centre alone, and that is not even counting all of the numerous state-run programmes. Indeed, the German government really wants you to learn German as soon as possible. For that reason, they even offer discount vouchers when you register as a foreigner. These vouchers can be put towards an integration course, which non-EU citizens generally have to complete in order to be eligible for permanent residency.

The language

It is especially tough for an English-speaking person to get to grips with the German language, as I found out first-hand. One aspect of this is linguistic complexity: the German language is very grammar-heavy. As you probably know by now, everything revolves around the three articles — *der, die* and *das*. You could say that your life depends on your ability to learn the correct usage of these articles; every subsequent conjugation is affected by it. Use *der* instead of *das* and, in the eyes of a native speaker, your whole sentence suddenly takes on a comical tone. They will either switch to English, or they just won't take you seriously.

Another aspect is pronunciation. German language is hard work — there are so many hissing sounds, the ones that are spelt with letters 'ch' — that it makes your head spin. In fact, you'll need to master two different 'ch' sounds: the hard 'ch', in words like *machen*, and the soft 'ch', in words like 'ich'. I won't bore you by going into detail as to why these are spoken differently. You'll learn that in your beginners classes sooner or later. Incidentally, the hissing sound is the main reason why German language sounds a bit *harsh* to foreigners. Understandably so — you can hardly describe someone hissing at you like an angry cat as friendly. It will take a considerable amount of time to adapt, and your ears might never fully get used to it. I can personally confirm this.

For a person from Scandinavia, German is much easier to learn, simply based on the fact that it stems from the same group of Nordic languages. But even if you're not from the land of Ikea, Smorgasbord, bacon and potatoes, don't be thrown off by all those dots on the letters. Naturally, I'm referring to the vowels 'Ä', 'Ö' and 'Ü'. A little footnote: I'm pretty sure that Scottish people have secretly incorporated those tricky Nordic vowels into their vocabulary by making them into one single sound — ÄÄÄOOOUUUUUIII. Nonetheless, all the consonant and vowel sounds put together will be very challenging for any foreigner who is determined to master *'Deutsch'*. No doubt, you'll be bending your tongue backwards and forwards trying to get the right word out of your mouth. All I can say is — don't give up.

There are countless memes about the German language out there: one in particular that springs to mind is a video of the same words being said in multiple different languages. As you might have already guessed, German words sound much harsher than their Italian, French, English or even Spanish counterparts. Thus, the word for a butterfly in German is *Schmetterling* — which sounds exactly how it is written. Similarly, the word for helicopter in German is *Hubschrauber* – pronounced HOOB-SCHRAU-BER. You can be forgiven for receiving a tiny jolt when you hear these words spoken out loud.

False friends

My first ever trip to Germany took place in 1999, when I was in sixth form. Our class had partnered up with a school in Geldern, a little-known town close to the Dutch border in the North Rhine-Westphalia region. At that particular time I was completely obsessed with Germany, and loved everything about it: the language, the culture, the food, and of course the German girls.[7] The little provincial town of Geldern was everything that the (North of) England was not, and I couldn't get enough of it. Of course, our exchange partners took us out partying, and I tried my best to show off all the vocabulary I had learnt by then. I should mention the fact that I was typically *right-brained.* In other words, I was very confident at speaking, had excellent pronunciation, and was not afraid of making mistakes. At the same time, I was terrible at grammar and syntax. The typical *left-brainer* is the other way around. Moreover, I was like a sponge, and tried to pick up every slang word — good or bad — that passed between my ears. One such word that I constantly heard young people say was 'Geil', pronounced 'Giyle'. It was the equivalent of 'cool' in English, my exchange partner told me. And so, before anyone could say supercalifragilisticexpialidocious (or, for our German readers — *Donaudampfschifffahrtselektrizitätenhauptbetriebswerkbauunterbeamtengesellschaft)* I was using the word left, right and centre. Unfortunately, there was a large pitfall waiting for me just round the corner. In hindsight, I should probably have done a bit more research prior to chimpanzee-ing the word like I did. I should mention to my millennial readers that all of this was before Google search, online dictionaries and smartphones. Anyway, we were at a party with lots of people, and I was in the mood to impress the

---

7   I'm not quite sure whether I should use the word girls or women. Historically they were seventeen, and yes, they were girls. On the other hand, at the time of writing this, I am thirty-eight, and it does feel a bit awkward.

German audience with my language skills. I wanted to tell everybody that I was cool, so I constructed the sentence as I would in English. I — AM — COOL, which in German equated to *Ich bin geil!* Little did I know that changing the object into a pronoun completely changed the meaning of the word *geil*. So, what I had actually said was, 'I am horny'. A thunderous torrent of laughter ensued, and there was nowhere to hide from my faux pas of the century. Moral of the story — if you're cool, be cool, *bruva*.

For those of you who have learnt some German at school — or are considering living in Germany and want to learn the language — it is important to know that there are some pitfalls in direct translations. In this section, I will list some of the important words that have different interpretations and should not be used literally. The most common confusions between German and English languages are caused by these 'false friends':

Diskutieren: Although it sounds like the English word 'to discuss', in German, the verb diskutieren is more commonly used to mean 'argue'. If you want to say 'discuss', it is better to use *besprechen*.

Sensibel: Another trap for the naïve student. *Sensibel* — which sounds like the English word 'sensible' — actually means 'sensitive'. The word for 'sensible' in German is *vernüftig*.

Bekommen: To get, to receive. The German word for the verb 'to become' is *werden*.

Spenden: To donate. The German word for 'to spend' is *ausgeben* (money), or *verbringen* (time).

Ich will (from wollen): I want. The German way of saying 'I will' would be *Ich werde.*

Der Chef/Die Chefin: The boss. The word for a 'chef' in German is *der Koch* (male) or *die Köchin* (female).

Das Gift: Poison. To say 'present', you'd need to use the word *das Geschenk.*

Die Rente: Pension. To say 'rent', the German word is *die Miete.*

Also: So, therefore. *Auch* is how you say 'also' in German.

Die Hochschule: College, university — not high school.

Die Dose: Can, tin. The German word for 'dose' is *die Dosis.*

Fast: Almost. *Schnell* is the German word for 'fast'.

die Note: Marks, grades. If you were going to make a note, the German word is *'die Notiz'.*

Die Kaution: Deposit. The German word for 'caution' is *die Vorsicht.*

Dick: Thick, fat. It's not my place to tell you how to say the other word in German.

Die Art: Kind, sort, manner. *Die Kunst* is how Germans talk about 'art'.

Du or Sie? Addressing people properly

A while ago, I received an email from an unknown person that began with the words *"Liebe Frau Fadi"*. An honest mistake, I'm sure. However, my eyes narrowed and I had to take a deep breath to refrain myself from hastily clicking reply and giving the sender a lecture on the fact that 'Fadi' is actually my first name, not to mention the fact that I'm a male homosapien. I wouldn't have been too bothered, had it only been an isolated incident. Unfortunately for me, I've lost count of the number of emails I've received where people have got my first and last names the wrong way around, and if I had replied to each and every one of these, I would probably still be typing furiously away. Granted, it's not like my name is Frank Gutentag, or something equally recognisable as 'a name' to a German. Even to an English person my name is quite confusing and I've often found myself reading an email with the greeting "Dear Gaziri". I guess I should thank my parents for picking two Arabic names. I've thought of indicating which is which in my email footer, but perhaps that would be a bit much.

The greater confusion begins when a person from the Anglo-Saxon world moves to the Germanic one. The reason being that in Germany people usually sign their emails with their last name. This also goes for greeting someone on the phone. If normal phone calls are not obsolete by the time this book is published, then you'll find that people in Germany simply answer the phone with their last name, not a 'hello', or any other form of greeting. As a novice to the German culture, this might be quite startling. It immediately sets a different tone to the conversation, a much more formal one, making you sit up straighter in your chair, clear your throat, and put up your guard, perhaps even making you wish you had written them an email instead. I remember the first time somebody answered the phone like this. I was taken aback, and promptly forgot everything I wanted to say. The key is to get used to it as quickly as possible, because, one way or another, it's gonna getcha, it's gonna getcha, getcha, getcha... Sorry, my mind wandered off there into a Blondie song for some reason. *Author clears throat*. As I was saying, the key is to get used to the formal greeting as quickly as possible, simply because you will have to endure lots and lots of formal interactions.

German etiquette demands that people use formal greetings in the workplace, particularly in large-scale multinationals, pretty much all municipal and government offices and in big German law firms, where archaic hierarchies and outdated ways stubbornly continue to defy the evolution process. On the other hand, the emergence of a myriad of 'creative' and 'exciting' start-ups across the country, with their 'flat hierarchies' and 'friendly' and 'informal' environments, is putting even this deep-seated pillar of German culture under immense pressure. Despite all of that, my guess is that the old German customs have still got a few generations before they disappear in favour of Googleisms, Appleisms, Anglicisms and many more *isms*.

A quick guide to addressing people in Germany

Do you know the person you're talking to?

No ⟶ Use Sie or their last name, if known. When introducing yourself, use either your full name or your last name. Don't use your first name on its own. Use the same formula for emails.

Yes ⟶ Are they your friend?

> **Yes** ⟶ You can use 'Du' and sign your emails with your first name.
>
> **No** ⟶ Use the same formal rules as laid out above.

Exception: You can call somebody by their first name in a formal setting, if they give you the 'signal'. This is usually a suggestion that you use *'Du'* (for instance, they might say, *"Lass uns duzen"*). As a rule of thumb, the person with higher seniority is the one who has to suggest this. For instance, if you're talking to your boss, you shouldn't casually suggest that you switch to *'Du'*, as you might find you're suddenly in the dog house, having the worst tasks dumped on your desk, and wondering what on earth you did wrong.

The 'weil' obsession

Once you've mastered the German language to a certain extent, you become a lot more tuned-in to the way people converse with each other. Remember how I rambled on about the Germans having a pathological obsession with explaining things, a deep-seated hatred of ambiguity, and an innate need for clarity? Well, part of that obsession extends into the German language.

One of the first times I encountered this 'German' phenomena was when I first moved to Hamburg in 2002 and met my first landlady — Belinda Nasenhuber, a 35-year-old single mum working as a television producer. I was renting a room in a spacious three-bedroom apartment where she lived with her two-year-old son in Altona — one of the popular Hamburg districts. She was originally from Bonn, which, of course, was once the capital of West Germany. One day, Belinda was supposed to give me the contract for the flat. But when I asked her about it, she hadn't yet got round to doing it. The response I got, however, sounded more like a final statement you get from the accused in a plea to the grand jury. It was certainly one of the longest explanations I have heard to date, and the attention to detail was astounding. I can't remember the exact transcript, but it went something like this:

Me: Hi, Belinda, do you have the rental contract we talked about?

Belinda: Oh no, I didn't manage to get it done today, BECAUSE I was at work and then my boss called me into the office and gave me more work, and then I had to spend the rest of the day on the phone to my colleagues, until it was very late, and then I had to wait for the right train from work, and it came late, so I got home much later than expected, and then I had to run out to the shops to buy food for Fabian (her son), because the shops close at 7pm, and he needs his food, otherwise he will get cranky and might get sick, and then I would have to take him to the doctors, and then I would be forced to take time off work, and so that's why I wasn't able to get your contract to you on time, but I will get it done tomorrow.

By the end of that sentence I expected her to be completely exhausted, with saliva dripping from her mouth, gasping for air and holding her knees like a boxer after twelve solid rounds. But she looked at me completely normally, expecting another follow up question, which, as you might have guessed, I never dared to ask — EVER AGAIN. After that 'first encounter' with the *extended weil clause',* as I call it, I had to endure many, many more.

At first I didn't pay too much attention to any of it, but gradually I became more and more agitated; like an innocuous rash you get on your elbow that you keep scratching, and it just gets worse and worse. As time went by, I became even more deeply engrossed in my examination of the German mindset, and finally began to understand the reasons behind this obsessive compulsion to give a trail of explanations after the simplest of excuses.

In a nutshell, the reason is twofold. On the one hand, it is rooted in German culture and the way you are expected to connect an action with the thing causing it. For example, if you want to say something simple like, "I'm going to the supermarket", most people would say just that, without the need to add anything else. To a German, however, that sentence in itself is incomplete, because it lacks an explicit root cause. So, a German would naturally add an explainer to that sentence: "... to get some food." You can apply this formula to pretty much anything: "I'm closing this door because it's cold," or "I'm lifting the teacup, so it doesn't get knocked over." Understanding this has helped me a lot in coping with the German mentality, and — on a more day-to-day level — it also explains why the Germans seem to be doing a live commentary on every single thing they do. The second reason is more complex, and it has to do with their uncertainty avoidance, a term coined by a Dutch sociologist Geert Hofstede, whose model we shall examine later in this book.

The tone

If you wanted to find an antithesis to the word 'charisma', the noun 'German' would not be far off. Whenever you talk to someone, it is imperative that your tone is calm, collected, even — quite frankly — absolutely boring. In fact, if someone is excited about something, you'd never be able detect it from their tone of voice. The same goes for expressing irritation or anger. There is very little variation in tone. So it is fair to say that the German language is fairly *monotone*. It's very rare to find anybody *animated* when they're talking. It almost seems like a taboo. Considering the fact that in the 1930s there were quite a few charismatic individuals, particularly in politics, who used the full range of their vocal chords, it is perhaps not difficult to see why such ways of speaking have fallen from grace, except, perhaps, in some populist quarters of the country.

The 'nein' word

In many cultures, people don't like being forced to commit to something, which is why they will always reply with a "maybe" or "let's see", or something in that vein. On the one hand, of course, there is a personality factor involved. Some people just don't like being pinned down. But there is undeniably a cultural element to this.

As we have established, the Germans like clarity and hate ambiguity. This translates into each and every part of their lives, and there is no better way to epitomise this than the way they talk. If you're a *fresher* in Germany, and have not yet been exposed to its customs to the full extent, then you are in for a treat. All you have to do is go down to your local bakery and ask if you can pay with a credit card. *"Nein!"* — Their response will reverberate in your ears. If you're not used to being spoken to like this, the words will sting like a wasp. They will sound hostile, punishing, and unforgiving, all at once. Forget your friendly "I'm sorry, but," or "I'm afraid," or any other form of politeness, chivalry or kindness (whether fake or not). None of that nonsense here. It took me more than a decade of constant *training* to finally get to grips with the 'N'-word. Even better, I've now finally come to understand why it is the way it is. The thing you have to get out of your head is, the Germans are not trying to be rude to you. On the contrary, they are trying to be as clear as possible, to make sure that there is not an iota of ambiguity in their answer. Unlike English speakers, the Germans do not have that fear of being *too direct.* In fact, I'm going to go further and state that, on the contrary, Germans are afraid of the opposite. Thus, in retrospect, you should try to see it as a positive: the louder and brassier the sound of the *'Nein!'*, the more helpful they are trying to be.

You might think of me as overly dramatic when I say this, but there are few cultures in the western world that clash more than the German and English worldviews and, having experienced both as a foreigner, I will try to explain why that is.

Apology accepted

Anybody who grew up in the UK, or was subjected to its colonisation at one stage or another — and yes I am talking about all the commonwealth countries — will know that apologising is more than simply saying you're sorry. It is not that easy to explain what the word 'sorry' is actually used for in the (British) English language, because it comes up in some many different situations. Of course, the English say "sorry" when they want to apologise for something that they've done: "Sorry I barged into you", "Sorry I missed your call", "Sorry I took the last piece of cake". The latter would actually never happen, because a British person would never take the last piece of cake (and would instead descend into a battle of chivalries with the words "No, you have it, please", "Oh, no, I'm already full from that scrumptious *Arrabiata*" and so on) — but you get the point.

But that's not the limit of British apologies - far from it. We seem to apologise for events in the universe that are far beyond the reach of a mere mortal, like one's own illness. If I said to my wife that I felt ill today, her initial response would be to say, "Sorry, my love." As if she could have done something to prevent it and was therefore solely responsible.

Another very important 'sorry' is used by the British when invading somebody's private space, like at a supermarket. If you see somebody standing in the deli section right in front of the olives you wish to purchase, you can reach for them, but you must make sure to utter the word "sorry" as you invade that person's private space. The same goes for crossing paths with strangers, or reaching for the elevator button at the same time as someone else, or being unsure of whether you are next in line: "Sorry, sorry, sorry!" This is considered a cornerstone of essential *Britishness*. In the US there is an added ingredient to that equation, namely a legal one. Without going too much into detail, basically anybody can sue anybody for almost anything. A woman whose coffee was too hot at McDonald's; a thief who slipped and broke his arm while robbing a house; and pretty much anyone who tries to tell the truth to the public about the *bad* multinational companies selling *cancer on a stick* and getting away with it. The word 'sorry' would thus come as a pre-emptive peace-maker to prevent anyone from shouting the by now standard phrase, "I'm gonna sue you!" Back to Britain, and on a deeper level, the word 'sorry' signifies your acknowledgement of another human being's existence in the same universe as yours. Subconsciously, you simply tell the other person, "I see you, you're one of us (humans), and I accept your gravitational mass as a simple truth."

In Germany, to put it bluntly, people never apologise. We've seen this phenomenon explained in the workplace chapter, and, essentially this *is the simple truth*. First of all, an apology can exist in only one possible scenario and that is if you've done some considerable harm to another person, be it physical or emotional. And by considerable harm, I mean a great amount of pain. Every other scenario is completely foreign to them. I would say that, in my seventeen years of living in Germany, this is still the thing I have struggled the most with getting used to. Somebody reaching over me at a buffet or a canteen — clearly invading my personal space — without saying so much as a single word, does tend to set off a mild nuclear explosion within me, and makes me want to erase that human being's physical body from this universe. This, of course, doesn't do me any good, and particularly doesn't help my passive aggressive side, which rages for at least another ten minutes. But, on the outside, my facial expression shows zero emotion. I won't move a single muscle and the only comment I'll mutter to myself is, "Bloody Germans."

This cultural difference is the main reason why the Brits consider the Germans *rude*. To a British person, the absence of "excuse me" and "sorry" equates to bad manners. But in German culture, this is not the case. Their *raison d'etre* is 'I am, therefore I can'. It would therefore be wrong to say that German people are rude, they are just... Germans. After all, we've already looked at their etiquette in elevators, or in public places, where there is a requirement to say "hello" and "goodbye". And, every now and then, when someone tries to squeeze past you on the bus, they will utter their equivalent of the British 'sorry': "*Einmal durch*", which literally translates as 'once through'.

Correcting people & Just criticism

If you're from one of these nations where saying 'sorry' ten times a day is simply par for the course, you will also know to be very careful when expressing any form of criticism or negative opinion in public. The use of language plays an important part in this, and the ability to *read between the lines* becomes an essential skill in order to decipher the actual meaning of what is being said.

The words and expressions used must be understating and anti-inflammatory. For example, if you're not happy with the situation you might say, "It's not ideal," and if you want to describe somebody who's being a bit of an arsehole, you are more likely to say that the person is "Not very pleasant," rather than calling them what they are. In fact, any form of directness is seen as a being negative, almost bolshy. Opinionated people full of emotions tend to be branded as antisocial, rude, and even vulgar.

For me, as a Brit, correcting others in public is an extremely delicate matter, so delicate in fact that I tend to steer clear of doing it altogether if I can. In extreme cases where a public correction becomes impossible to avoid, whether in a professional setting or a social one, you must swerve delicately between numerous pitfalls, to avoid being branded as *rude*. Not just that, but you must always be painstakingly tactful and polite, or else you'll find yourself on thin ice very quickly. It is a bit like walking on eggshells.

Bearing that in mind, you couldn't end up with a more contrasting mindset than that of the Germans. For them, correcting people is an essential part of being that every citizen must partake in. Some even consider it their moral duty, because, quite frankly, if something's wrong, then it's not right. As we have seen in previous chapters, some of the cornerstones of *being German* are being precise and unambiguous, offering lengthy and detailed explanations, and having a high moral responsibility, which loosely translates into *minding everyone else's business.* In other words, if something is wrong, it must be pointed out: polite or not, in public or in private. It is essential to get your head around this, if you are ever going to understand why complete strangers have the audacity to tell you off in public, or tell you that *you are wrong,* because they think so. The same applies to criticising people. I remember the first time a complete stranger in the shape of an elderly woman lectured me outside our flat on the topic of recycling. I think my cardinal sin was to place a green bottle into the container for the brown bottles. She seemed appalled by my actions, and grilled me for about five minutes on a range of topics that spanned from environmental issues through to the *Hausordnung* (the house rules or 'neighbours' conduct', which is usually appended to rental agreements in Germany). According to her, if I had read this document more carefully, I would have been better informed.

The big question is — *where* does this moral obligation come from? The short answer — their education. From an early age, German pupils are taught the value of expressing their opinion, and, equally, of listening to others expressing theirs. It's part of the German social etiquette. And telling somebody that they are wrong is not considered impolite at all, even in public. More on this in Chapter 7, but for now, I'll just leave it at that.

Terminology - Don't get it wrong

As I mentioned earlier, German language is extremely logical, and for that reason there's nothing worse than getting your terminology wrong. For instance, we've seen how in the *Baumarkt*, where every bolt and screw has its own name, you have to come prepared, or face your own demise. Well, the bad news is, it's pretty much the same in every sector in Germany — no matter whether you are talking to a bank manager, an engineer, a doctor, or a tax consultant. Without proper terminology, you won't get very far. The good news – well, actually, there is none. As my Aussie mate would say, "You're facked, mate."

The professional institutions are particularly unforgiving of the use of wrong terminology. By now, you're familiar with Germany's love of a compound noun, so it should come as no surprise that a visit to one of these establishments will throw up a whole load of very complex terms that, to the naked eye, seem very similar, but actually mean very different things. And so, just like the example at the home depot store, when going to government offices be sure to brush up on all the different terms that are used in connection with what you are there to do. *Bescheinigungen, Erklärungen, Verpflichtungen, Anmeldungen, Beglaubigungen, Qualifizierungen, Anpassungen, Zeugnisse, Bestätigungen, Bescheide and Urkunde* — and that's barely even scratching the surface. All of those are types of documents that are 'same same, but different'. Imagine the joy when you realise that those already complicated words can be compounded with other complicated words to make them all even more complicated. Hurray! And so it pays to do your homework, so that the minute you're asked for your *Meldebestätigung, Verpflichtungserklärung, Heiratsurkunde, Führungszeugnis* or any other ultra-specific document, you can whip it out at the drop of a hat.

> **Good to know:**
>
> *Whereas the English language is very relaxed when trying to explain something — you can definitely get away with saying, "I need that thing for my passport," or "I need that bit of paper for my application" and still be met with a helpful response like "Oh you mean a residency permit" — in German, unless you know exactly which type of document you are after, you will have no such luck. Most likely, you will get a bewildered blank stare in your direction, followed by a lecture to the tune of, "Did you not read through the guidelines on our website?" And with that, they will refer you to those horrible German government sites, which might as well be written in Sanskrit — pages upon pages of text in tiny font, completely unreadable, impossible to navigate.[8]*

---

8   In their defence, Germany has made a great push for digitisation in the past year or so. Particularly in their public service sector, they've made a real effort to update and declutter their websites, and make them more user-friendly.

Words that only exist in German

And now that you have mastered not only the intricacies of the German language itself, but also how it's used in everyday life, it's time to learn some *really German* German. And by that I mean, there are words in the German language that cannot be found in any other language, partly due to their originality, and partly due to the weird combination of nouns – a bit like putting a Coke and a Fanta in one bottle, if you ask me (yes, the Germans do that, and we will come back to this in the next chapter). Some of these words have been adopted in other languages as well, like *Zeitgeist, Schadenfreude* and *Kindergarten,* to name a few off the top of my head, but most will forever remain within the German borders, and it's not difficult to see why. Below, I've listed some of the most common ones you're likely to encounter in your everyday surroundings.

Fremdschämen (alien embarrassment): Feeling embarrassed on somebody else's behalf.

Ohrwurm (ear worm): Having an annoying/catchy melody stuck in your head for long periods of time. Anybody who has ever experienced this can attest to just how annoying the Ohrwurm can be.

Erklärungsnot (explanation emergency): Having the urge to explain everything, without anyone asking for it.

Zungenbrecher (tongue breaker): A difficult to pronounce word or sentence which literally causes your tongue to 'break'. German's got plenty of 'em.

Spassvogel (fun bird): Makes little sense in English, but in German it is commonly used to describe somebody who likes a bit of a laugh.

Klugscheißer (smart shitter): Another expression that makes little or no sense in English, if translated literally. In German, the expression is used to discribe somebody who is a smart-ass.

Kuddelmuddel (muddled mess): Describes chaos or mess and is pronounced exactly as it is written. Other synonyms in German include *Mischmasch* and *Kladderadatsch*.

Kopfkino (head cinema): Mentally playing out an entire scene in your mind, as if in a movie theatre.

Luftschloss (air castle): An impossible or unrealistic dream — like building a castle in the air — used to describe something unattainable.

Weichei (soft egg): A weak person, a wimp.

Eselsbrücke (donkey's bridge): A mnemonic, i.e. a system or pattern of letters that helps you remember information.

Kummerspeck (worry bacon): Weight gained through comfort eating.

Innerer Schweinehund (inner pig-dog): The little devil on your shoulder. In most cases you can blame your inner pig-dog as a completely different entity to yourself.

Torschlusspanik (closing-gate panic): The feeling of panic with added time pressure.

Sitzfleisch (sit or seat meat): Somebody able to sit through hard or boring meetings, parties or speeches —

basically because they carry their own cushion or "seat meat".

Vorfreude (pre-excitement): The period just before you get excited or happy

Vorentscheidung (pre-decision): The time period just before a decision is made.

Fancy a tongue-twister?

If you think highly of your German skills, have a go at some of these *Zungenbrecher* below. Go on, I dare you!

- Fischers Fritz fischt frische Fische. Frische Fische fischt Fischers Fritz
- Zwischen zwei Zwiebeln zwischen zwei Schlangen.
- Acht alte Ameisen aßen am Abend Ananas.
- Wilde Wiesel wollten wissen wo warme Würstchen wachsen.
- Kleine Kinder können keine Kirsch-Kerne knacken.
- Blaukraut bleibt Blaukraut und Brautkleid bleibt Brautkleid
- Esel essen Nesseln nicht. Nesseln essen Esel nicht.
- Schweizer Schwert Schweißer schweißen Schweizer Schwerte, Schweizer Schwerte schweißen Schweitzer Schwertschweißer
- Schneiders Scheren schneiden scharf, scharf schneiden Schneiders Scheren.

Chapter 4
Food & Leisure

As you have gathered by now, Germans are very serious people; they take their work, their social responsibilities, and their language, all very seriously indeed. As a natural progression from that, they also take their leisure and recreation time very seriously. As we shall discover in this chapter, they invest a lot of their time planning 'free time', in order to 'get the most' out of it. And if you think that 'church' and 'Sunday breakfast' are the only things occupying the calendars of all *good* Germans, then you are in for another treat – known as Tatort, which occupies the eight pm Sunday slot of *all* federal republicans.

Aside from leisurely activities, Germans are also serious about food. It's not famous for it, but Germany actually has a rich food tradition, which goes back more than 1500 years. It has great diversity too, owing to its geographical location, bordered by no fewer than nine countries, and of course the sea: the Scandinavian and maritime influence up north; the Eastern European influence to the east; the French and the Dutch in the west; and of course a whole pot of countries across the Alps to the south. This explains the great diversity of culinary specialities, depending on where in Germany you are, and as such, this topic undoubtedly deserves a book of its own; or even a whole chapter. And, indeed, most book shops in Germany will have a culinary section dedicated solely to German food. Since this is not the actual aim of this book, I am merely going to touch upon a few bits that have stuck in my memory — both good and bad — to let the naïve, unsuspecting expat know what they're in for.

Ein Currywurst mit Pommes, bitte!

When I lived in Berlin between 2015 and 2018 I witnessed something I will never, ever forget. It was the sight of a French man (I know he was French, because he was in the queue ahead of me talking to his missus), being handed the *Currywurst* he had just ordered, with the words "Enjoy your meal". He looked like he had just been given a brick. He stared, bewildered, at a piece of sausage on his little white cardboard plate. It had some brownish sauce on it, with a little yellow powder sprinkled on top, and was accompanied by a slice of plain white bread. He was not amused. But since he was obviously a tourist — and tourists do what tourists do (i.e. try local cuisine, explore the local spots, submerge themselves into the local culture, cuisine and music scene) — he decided to embrace the experience. With a shug of, "Ah, what the heck," he tried it anyway. The moment he bit into the sausage, however, his facial expression turned into a barely detectable grimace. Not the kind you see when someone bites into a lemon. Instead, it was more akin to somebody biting into a sour grape, or eating a nut that has gone off. The kind of shock your body gets when the expectations projected from the visuals do not coincide with the information your taste buds are sending back. I chuckled quietly to myself and thought the guy should have probably inquired about the brownish sauce and the yellowish powder before consuming it. And then I thought back to my own experience of trying a *Currywurst* for the first time. It was pretty much the same. My brain was trying to compute and equate the sensation my taste buds were transmitting to it, but all in vain.

In fact, that brownish sauce is known as *curry-ketch-up,* and the yellowish powder is curry powder. There is a whole institution behind the preparation of the *Curry-wurst*, which the kiosk owner will be more than happy to explain to you. This is particularly the case for a *Berlin-er* (a person from Berlin, not a doughnut). Everyone will have their own favourite kiosk and, if needs must, they would be prepared to defend their opinion to the death. This German *delicacy* is sold — without fail — at every train station, football stadium, concert hall, tourist at-traction and museum in the country — basically, wher-ever large crowds gather. There are even some restau-rants that specialise in *Currywurst*, served usually with a healthy portion of *Pommes* (French fries) and — natural-ly — curry-ketchup. Yes, you heard correctly — it is called that, because ketchup in Germany is curry-flavoured by default. In order to get a normal, non curry-flavoured ketchup with your fries, you would have to specify that to the waiter. *"Guten Appetit!"*

Franzbrötchen

Every nation in the world has got a typical *morning snack,* something people grab from the bakery on their way to work. In the UK, it could be a pasty or a sausage roll; in France it's a croissant; and in the Middle East it might be baked flat bread with thyme paste. In Germany —

or more precisely, in Northern Germany — the equivalent of a morning snack is called a *Franzbrötchen*. This is a thinly-sliced cinnamon-flavoured pastry, about the size of a croissant. It is hugely popular and comes in all kinds of different varieties. Aside from its original flavour, you can also purchase ones made with *dinkelmehl* - a healthier, dark rye flour. It is also available with different toppings like caramel, nuts, sesame seeds, cardamom, and a plethora of other permutations. A little weird-tasting at first, you'll probably dismiss it as mundane or average, but as time goes by (song reference intended), you'll notice how it grows on you. My personal favorite is the dinkel-sesam variety, which is actually quite hard to find. Perhaps I have an acquired taste — even by German standards.

Weird foods: *The Spezi*

Of all the weird food inventions I've encountered in Germany — and there are plenty, including the emblematic *Currywurst*; the cheeky *Bananenweizen* (a wheat beer made with banana juice); the vomitous looking *Labskaus* (a mixture of corned beef, fried egg, pickled herring, gherkin and beetroot); and the non-alcoholic beer (speaks for itself) — the strangest one to date remains the so-called *Spezi* — basically a Fanta and a Coke put in one bottle. I can't for the life of me comprehend how somebody thought this would be a great idea. It was either a product invented purely by a mistake, perhaps when someone too drunk to know any better accidentally poured the remains of a Coke bottle into a glass of Fanta, and decided to drink it anyway. Otherwise, it must be a product of German waste efficiency — somebody who desperately wanted to cash in on the bottle by recycling it at the store (and so receive their 25-cent *Pfand* deposit back), but at the same time didn't want to throw away half a bottle of Coke. Whatever its origins, and whichever way you look at it, it tastes revolting, and you can imagine what it does to your stomach, once it finds its way down there.

Spargelzeit

Every nation has its weird food obsession that is baffling to the outsiders. In France it's the baguette; in England, it's fish and chips; in Hungary they have their traditional *Goulash*, and in Germany you might instinctively think of the German sausage. But, although the sausage is a German obsession, there is another — perhaps lesser well-known one — that sets German pulses racing every spring. I'm talking, of course, about white asparagus season. From mid-April until approximately the end of June, Germans get into a frenzy of buying this seemingly average-looking (and tasting) vegetable, with great emphasis put on locally grown produce. Supermarkets, farmer's markets, restaurants and pretty much everyone in the food business will put up big signs advertising the *Spargel aus der Region* (locally grown asparagus) and create lots of pomp and circumstance around this limp and rather unspectacular piece of veg. You're likely to see asparagus soup listed on a fair few menus, but the Germans' favourite way to eat it is characteristically indulgent: served with parma ham and new potatoes, and topped with a generous portion of hollandaise sauce.

At the restaurant

As we've already seen, getting used to the service at German supermarkets or on the phone is one thing — but getting to grips with the way waiters and waitresses operate in this country is a whole different story. Over the years, it's been bothering me to the point of (occasional) rage: the kind that makes you want to pick up a grenade launcher and go on a shooting spree. This might sound a bit dramatic, and I implore you not to read into this all too seriously, but, in my opinion, few things are worse than being at a restaurant where the service is *bad*. And, unfortunately, it's rare to find a German restaurant where the service *isn't* bad. Let me explain.

First of all, it is of utmost importance to take Germanness into account. In other words, as we have already learnt, there is a difference between what is seen as *friendly* in the UK and in Germany, with the latter tending to be less fussy about the way they are addressed, the language used, and the *pleases* and *thank yous*. So, in order to show the full extent of my vexation on this topic, I will need to split restaurant service into different criteria — and point out exactly where Germany fails at providing an adequate service:

Friendliness and welcoming manner: When going to a restaurant, be it a little Asian budget place, or a posh bistro serving *cordon bleu,* you always want to feel welcome when you first arrive. A simple 'hello' from any member of staff will suffice, with bonus points given to attentive staff who greet you and ask you how they can be of help. In Germany, you can expect to be greeted, and then asked how many people would like to be seated e.g. "A table for two?" If you're unlucky, you might have to stand around for several minutes before even being acknowledged, but, whatever you do, do not go and pick a table yourself.

Response time and attentiveness: Once seated, depending on the place, you might find that there aren't any menus on the table. Be sure to check immediately, and signal to the waiter if there aren't any. If you don't, you might be waiting a long time for them to be brought to the table. It's not as self-explanatory as you might think.

Ordering: If you've got the menus and you see the waiter coming towards you, be sure you've selected the dishes you want. If the dishes have numbers, it would be more efficient to just say the number you want. Remember — German waiters will not banter with the guests; when they come to you, it's ordering time. Expect a short prompt sentence like *"Was darf's sein?"* (What will it be?) A sure way to get the waiter annoyed is to start asking questions about the food. And, although this is common in other cultures, a German brain will be close to exploding if you ask them if the chicken risotto is good, or even worse, asking what they think is better, the *Wiener Schnitzel* or the *Rostbratwurst*? These are absolute no-nos in a German restaurant. Best case scenario: They will tell you that the selection is 'subjective' depending on each individual and their taste. Worst case: They will tell you that they will come back in a few minutes, when you have managed to narrow down your choice to *One Dish*. In such a case, expect to be waiting for a long time.

Making switches: Do not ask to switch the garnish in a preset menu. For example, substituting boiled potatoes for chips or visa versa (unless this is explicitly stated as an option on the menu). Requesting to do so will earn you nothing more than a stern "no".

Questions: Do not ask the waiter questions which are already answered in the menu, such as whether the steak comes with a side dish. Best case scenario, they'll tell you the options, adding, "as is written in the menu" (which, in case you didn't realise, is a small dig at you for not having read the menu diligently yourself). Worst case, they'll ask you to refer to the menu page 'XY'. Or worst case: they'll ask you to look in the menu on page 'XY'.

Ability to deal with 'annoying' questions such as "I ordered my drink 10 minutes ago": If your drink hasn't arrived and you are remonstrating this to the waiter or waitress, you might be shocked to hear that he or she will start complaining about the lack of staff they have at the joint, the fact that there are so many guests, or even outright scolding you for being impatient. "Show some empathy toward the poor waiter, you ignorant customer!"

Check-ins: Once you've got your food, there is a custom which works like clockwork in Germany. After approximately five minutes, the waiter will come around and ask if the food tastes 'okay'. Although a seemingly polite gesture, it merely serves as just that — a polite gesture. The last thing they'll expect is for you to say something other than, "Yes, everything is in good order." In fact, I've tested this myself by replying "Nein," only for the waiter to not even register my answer, trotting along on autopilot, oblivious to any deviation from the *routine*. It is quite astonishing, but the only place where Germans don't complain — is at the restaurant.

Payment: When you ask for the bill, the first question you'll hear in response (if there are two or more people in your party) is if you are paying together. Waiters hate split-bill payments, even though in 99.9 percent of cases, people in groups do pay separately. If that's the case, giving a bigger tip goes without saying. It is also worth noting that a lot of restaurants will only accept cash — yes, you heard me. So make sure you bring a wad of cash with you, or at least ask the waiter whether they take cards, before you sit down for your scrumptious meal.

Customers are always right: If you're in Germany, you can forget this mantra. You're not in one of your episodes of *How I Met Your Mother.* In fact, you're not in the US at all. Neither are you in the UK, the Middle East or Asia. In other words, make sure you follow the rules, order when the waiter comes around, shove your food down your gob, pay together — in cash — and bugger off. Oh, and don't forget to leave a sterling review on Google.

In all fairness, a good proportion of Germans constantly complain about the service at the restaurants. There is a difference between them and expats though, and it can easily be detected in their tone if you pay attention. In contrast to a foreigner, who retorts in a quasi suspended sense of — shall we say — disbelief, having just woken up from a nightmare, when you hear a German person complaining about the service at the restaurant, you can detect a touch aura of resignation in their voice. Akin to a natural element like the weather, rain, or taxes. Sure, they dislike it, but there's absolutely nothing you, they or anyone can do about it — so just go back to point i) and repeat!

Quality of service, by countries visited:

1. The Emirates (Dubai, Abu Dhabi, Doha)
2. Russia
3. The USA and Canada
4. Middle East and North Africa (Lebanon, Egypt, Morocco)
5. Poland, Hungary, Czech Republic
6. The UK
7. Italy
8. Iberia (Spain, Portugal)
9. Scandinavia (Iceland, Sweden, Norway, Denmark)
10. Germany
11. France

The Flohmarkt

Every Saturday in Germany, thousands of outdoor spaces are filled with flea markets, where people sell all kinds of junk that has been collecting dust for years in their attic or garage: I'm talking anything and everything, from silverware, tupperware, clothes and furniture, to musical instruments, plants, lamps, bicycles, old DVDs and car stereos. It's the German equivalent of a car boot sale in the UK. There is, however, one major difference: Haggling in Germany is an alien concept. It's simply not done — and people don't know how to do it. And thus if someone says thirty euros, this is actually the price they want to get. No point wasting your breath on starting with a half-price offer and then going up to what you're actually prepared to pay for the item, which is de facto part of the fun itself. It amazes me, but it seems as though they would much rather take the junk back to their garage than sell below the asking price. And the same goes in a reverse situation: if you're asking for thirty euros for an item, they will not haggle with you; instead they will just politely say something like, "Ah ok, well then maybe not," and proceed to the next stand. This strange rule applies unilaterally on all platforms. Whether you're at the flea market, on *eBay Kleinanzeige* (the German version of Ebay), on Facebook Marketplace, you name it. I was so curious about this concept that I did a bit of comparative research. I placed an IKEA sofa-bed on Facebook Marketplace in two different locations: one in Hamburg, and the other one in Northwich, a town in the UK. The price was inflated for a second-hand sofa, but it was in a very good condition. Next to the price I put 'or near offer'; in Germany, you have to tick an extra box for this which says *Verhandlungsbasis* (price negotiable). Straight away, I was inundated by messages from UK accounts asking about the sofa, if I'd take XY amount, and some really cheeky, ridiculously low offers. In Germany, not even one message. The only plausible excuse I can find for this is that the Germans will have thought long and hard about the price before they set their minds on it: the wear and tear, emotional value, current market value and so on, and thus the price they arrive at is absolutely final, take it or leave it.

"How much for this watch?"
"30 euros."
"Okay, how about 20?"
"NEIN!"
"25?"
"NEIN!"
"29.50?"
"NEIN!"
"Okay, I'll give you 30 as you asked."
"NEIN!"

At the bakery

There are few places that encompass German culture as well as a traditional Bäckerei — the bakery. And, to illustrate this point, I've written a very probable dialogue that anyone will have experienced when going down to the bakery, either in Germany, or in the UK. Both the customer and the shop-keeper are faced with the exact same scenario. The responses, while very different, are equally culturally acceptable.

English shop keeper: "Hi there, can I help you?"
German shop assistant: "Next!"

English customer: "Oh hi, can I have two sausage rolls please?"
German customer: "Two *Salzstangen* to take out!"

English shop keeper: "Oh I'm sorry, but we've just run out."
German shopkeeper: "No, we don't have any!"

English customer: "Oh, ok, I'll have two cheese pasties then please."
German customer: "Then I take two *Käsestangen.*"

English shop keeper: "There you go, will that be all?"
German shopkeeper: "Another wish?!"

English customer: "No, that's it, thank you."
German customer: "No thanks!"

English shop keeper: "That's two pounds fifty, please."
German shopkeeper: "Two fifty!"

English customer: "Have you got a change for a twenty pound note?"
German customer: "I only have a twenty euro note."

English shop keeper: "Oh, have you got anything smaller?"
German shopkeeper, shaking their head: "I can't give change, it's the end of the shift and I've given all of my change to the last person. You should bring some small change with you when going to a bakery!"

English customer: "Afraid not."
German customer: "I know, but today after I took my kids to school, I went to the bank, as I usually do to get money out, and the machine only gave me twenty euro denom-

inations, whereas normally it would give me ten and five euros notes."

English shop keeper, shouting to co-worker: "Tilly! Have you got change for a twenty pound note?"
German shopkeeper: Roll eyes and starts rummaging in till, obviously annoyed.

Now, imagine what happens if you pair the English customer with a German shopkeeper, or vice versa. Precisely! A cultural meltdown, whichever way you try to spin this one.

On holiday

The first thing you notice when you get off the plane anywhere outside of Germany is usually how bloody friendly everyone is: smiling, saying hello, not avoiding eye contact. And I'm not talking about countries on the other side of the world where indigenous villagers with ivory bones in their noses come running from bamboo cuts to greet the mysterious foreigner. No, I'm talking about neighbouring countries like Sweden, Denmark, Poland, or Hungary. It's not that I'm complaining about Germans being naturally unfriendly — not at all. I'm just saying that over the years I've been conditioned to accept — shall we say — a different way of communicating, one that bypasses all unnecessary coquettishness, pleasantries and forthcoming behaviour that has been nurtured in other European countries for centuries. As we've already established, it's not that people are impolite in Germany, not at all. It's just that all pleasantries in Germany are deemed as being 'superfluous to requirements'.

Every holiday I've been on so far, my number one priority has always been the same — get as far away from *ze Germans* as I possibly can. This might sound very anti-German, and, in a way, it probably is. But, then again, a lot of readers will probably agree with me: whether you're from Hamburg or Norfolk, Gothenburg or Paris, the last thing you'd want is to take your home surroundings (and people) with you to the beautiful shores of Greece, or Spain, or wherever it is that you're going. The very essence of the word *holiday* is to take a break from everything that reminds you of your home surroundings. And to me that means taking a break from Germany, its people, its language, its idiosyncrasies, its naked saunas (more on those later), and so on and so forth. Even though I do take great care in trying to avoid the German tourist spots, you can never be 100 percent certain, and if you're travelling to all the charter destinations, the probability is high that you'll find yourself having a *close encounter* with a German person. This has happened to me a few times, but luckily I just pretend that I don't speak a word of German, and if anyone tries talking to me, I just smile at them and tell them in my Queen's English that I don't understand a word they are uttering. If you thought that the Brits were

rude by assuming everybody speaks English on holiday —
be it Spain, Portugal, Marrakesh or Timbuktu — German
tourists have reached the same degree of ignorance, and
perhaps have even surpassed it (perhaps this should not
be that much of a surprise to the Greeks, the Spanish, the
Poles, or even the Portuguese, considering the fact that
Germany accounts for one of their biggest exporting destinations. Moreover, as in the case of Greece, let's not forget that Germany more or less bailed out the whole country when it was on the brink of a collapse. I've lost count
at the number of times that I have seen German tourists
shouting at poor waiters in German, baffled by the fact
that those *ignorant* Spaniards cannot understand their
perfectly enunciated *Reichsdeutsch*.

At this point, I do have to back-peddle a bit. Granted, not all tourists are like that, but there's a good share
of *bad apples* in every charter destination. The interesting
thing is this: Germans do tend to hoard together; thus,
you will often find hotels that cater specifically for German clientele. All of their signs will be written in German; their activity guides are required to speak German;
and even their musicians are told to play German songs. I
guess it is comforting to go abroad safe in the knowledge
that people will understand you, and can be relied upon
to know that 7am means exactly that, and not a minute
later. With large-scale holiday operators like Robinson
or TUI, you will probably find that most of the client-fac-
ing staff are German, Austrian or Swiss themselves. The
reason is simple: Germans are the best at understanding

their fellow citizens' quirks and expectations when on holiday. Which brings me to my next point: what Germans want to get out of their holiday.

Planning is everything. My ideal way of spending a holiday would be to sleep in late, get up when I want to, have a late breakfast with at least two cups of coffee, and then figure out what to do with the rest of the day. Perhaps I'll go on a hike, or take a dip in the sea. If I get bored with one setting I might get up early the next day to do a longer day trip. Either way, there is no pressure to get anything done and those *Carpe Diem* bashers can go and 'f*ck themselves'. I'm on holiday.

What I just described to you would be a total nightmare for a German person. They would be literally rocking back and forth, shivering in cold sweat at the sheer thought of being subjected to such a laughable imitation of a 'holiday'. The German mantra is that holiday time is precious time that must be utilised to its fullest. And thus, planning is essential.

It is worth mentioning at this stage that Germans enjoy some of the most generous holiday allowances in Europe. If you have lived in other countries before you came to Germany, you'll notice that people in this country enjoy great benefits. These include up to thirty days of vacation per year, on top of approximately national and regional public holidays. Most of these are religious and related to the Christian faith. *Labour Day* on 1st May celebrates workers, their rights, and their contributions to society and the economy, while *German Unity Day* on 3rd October commemorates the Reunification of Germany on that same day in 1990. Depending on the federal state you live in, you could have anything between ten and thirteen additional days off per year. Statistically speaking, people in Bavaria have the most national holidays.

But having lots of holiday days is no excuse to squander them willy nilly. So, the perfect German holiday day would start with a wakeup call from your hotel at around seven or eight in the morning. You're probably in Majorca. You would make your way down to the beach (or pool) and reserve your sun lounger for the day before heading in for your breakfast. This is best achieved by placing a towel on top of it.

A good friend of mine (let's call her *Brunhilde* for the sake of anonymity) is the epitome of the German tourist. Last year, I agreed to join her and her family on their annual vacation in Corfu. It was a beautiful stretch of beach on the northern part of the island. They've been going to the same place for almost fifteen years now, always staying at the same guesthouse, always in the same double room, eating at the same restaurant and drinking at the same bar. They are on first-name terms with the owners of the guesthouse, the restaurant, and the bar, and they get priority service everywhere they go. On my last night there, we all went for a meal. When the waiter came and asked if we were ready, people started ordering food and drinks. At one point, someone hesitated, and so I seized the gap to jump in and place my order —only to be scolded in a full public shaming by Brunhilde. Apparently this was against the clockwise ordering tradition they had been perfecting for the past eighteen years and I was promptly put in my place. A year on, I still feel the lump in my throat.

I almost forgot to mention one important thing about German tourists: a lot of holiday destinations are virtually exclusively financed through them. They book earlier than anyone else, they never behave badly, and they always pay without asking any questions. Take last year's trip to Corfu with my German friends, for example. The whole resort was filled with Germans and that was pretty much it for diversity. The local supermarket was almost entirely stocked with products from Aldi and other German brands. The ingredients lists on the back of the packaging were all written — naturally — in German.

I was curious to see what the locals thought of German tourists, so I asked the owner of a guest house where we were staying. His take on the subject was that Germans were probably the best guests out of all the nations he's dealt with. He pointed to their reliability, punctuality with payment, their general behaviour on premises, their hygiene, and their extra spending as the main reasons. He also mentioned the fact that, if they like the resort, they tend to return year after year, with some of his customers having holidayed there for fifteen years on the trot.

Incidentally, he mentioned the Brits as being the worst kind of tourists, but did not elaborate. Judging by his previous criteria, one can deduce that they are unreliable guests who don't pay, behave like idiots, trash the place, and don't spend a penny on anything extra. Actually, that does sound familiar.

Allotments

Although it might not be the first thing that comes to your mind when thinking of a holiday, you will find that Germans are very fond of their allotments — little plots of land they rent for recreational purposes only. And you'll be surprised to find that many citizens will gladly swap a beach in Mallorca in favour of getting their hands dirty on the outskirts of their own town. In cities like Berlin, Hamburg and Munich in particular, where people live in urban areas in close proximity, these inexpensive escapes offer a good alternative to owning your own garden. The German word for it is *Kleingartenverein*, a small garden club. As the name suggests, it's a club, and in order to become a member you have to apply and join a long list of hopefuls. This membership — designed by Germans for Germans — has a long list of rules and regulations attached to it. Moreover, these regulations are written in the German lawbook and form part of the German constitution. As it happens, I came across one of these contracts not so long ago. Aside from precise measurements of how big your shed is allowed to be built, I noted some other interesting things. For example, it states that one third of your garden has to be used for planting fruit and vegetables for your own use. Another rule states that all members of the club must do some chores around the club, i.e. outside of your own little plot. This could include mowing the lawn, minor repair works, or painting benches. In other words, if you think you can just relax and put your feet up, you are mistaken. You better think twice before getting yourself into it. Your tea and biscuits have to be earned first, the German way.

Recreation

Germans love recreation. They love doing sports, going to the gym, general fitness classes, power workouts, swimming, and pretty much anything that allows them to burn off the calories acquired while sitting in the office, eating bratwurst and drinking delicious beer. Unlike the Brits, however, they are not obsessed with building muscle in their upper body — at least not as evidently as back in Blighty. Their aim is purely to maintain their fitness levels and have a healthy and well-balanced lifestyle. One thing that is absolutely certain about the *German way* of life is their obsession with forming clubs — the so-called *Verein*.

There is an abundance of widespread jokes about this, even amongst Germans themselves. It goes something like this:

"What happens when more than two people meet up to play sports?"

"They start a club."

Although this is slightly exaggerated, the gist of it is true indeed. To the unassuming expat, this may seem a bit *odd*. "Why cause so much fuss about getting together to kick a ball around a park?" But, to Germans, this makes perfect sense. The biggest incentive being the fact that a *Verein* is an officially-registered non-profit organisation, which can benefit from all the perks of being not-for-profit, in the same way a charity does. Another thing we can't exclude — in light of the German obsession with insurance — is the fact that anyone who gets injured while playing as part of a *Verein*, be it a tiny scratch on one's elbow, a nosebleed, or any *proper* injury, would be covered by insurance, under a similar law to the one that ensures that employees are covered by a company's insurance policy.

In all the years I've been in Germany I've been involved in many different clubs focused on different sports, including football, Scandinavian floorball, gym workouts, swimming and power workouts. Over the years, I've noticed that Germans need a lot more information about what they are doing, and above all *why* they are doing it. Take a regular spinning class as an example. There really isn't that much of a science behind it. You get on a bike, adjust the seat, and — off you go, pedalling away your calories to some trance beat that gets your adrenaline pumping. You'd be surprised to know that, if you go to a beginner's class in Germany, the instructor will spend a good ten minutes explaining everything — useful or not — from how to adjust the seat so that it matches the distance between the seat and handlebars, to what slopes you'll tackle during the session, what speed you're going to reach, and even what to do if you get tired. "I mean really?! Come on now! I'm sure that I'll be able to figure out for myself that if I get tired, I'll either reduce the resistance, or get off the bloody bike." You might think that, but there is absolutely no use in trying to convey this to the instructor. And you'll make things ten times worse for yourself if you — god forbid — crack a joke about it. So, after years of trial and error, I discovered that the best thing to do is to just tell them that you're an experienced rider, and they'll leave you in peace.

One of the striking things I've noticed about German men in particular, particularly in reference to competitive sports, is their complete and utter lack of any concept of manning up — a term that I grew up with as a kid (now slightly outdated, but I can't think of a better one, so I hope the reader will excuse me), which includes things like not whining in general, and especially not if you fall over. So you get up and get on with it. You pretend not to notice the scratch on your elbow, and if you get a proper gash, you'll barely even acknowledge it, saying something like, "Oh, it's just a scratch." With this in mind, it's very hard for me to accept people who do complain about such trivial things. I've never heard more people complain about being ill or getting mildly injured as I have here in Germany, which they customarily do to make other people take pity on them.

Every Thursday night, I go to play squash at a fitness club called the *Kaifu* Lodge. It's quite a snazzy place with fancy workout rooms with designer spotlights, massive TV screens and the latest fitness machines. The place also has a spa, filled with saunas, swimming pools, steam rooms, and *quiet rooms* — yes, quiet rooms, as in rooms where people read books, relax, or even sleep. All the people there look like they had just stepped out of a Tommy Hilfiger catalogue: all under 35, super fit, in the shape of their lifetime, wearing the latest Nike and New Balance gear, frollicking around the place with their wireless Bose headphones, sipping their smoothies, or whatever it is that they have in those flasks with the recycled paper straws. Unfortunately, the squash corner is anything but... what I just described. It is filled with old(er) men over the age of fifty-five, whose breath could kill a medium-sized gerbil, wearing shorts that were fashionable in the seventies, sweating profusely next to me on the court. To add salt to the wound — these *old men* are bloody good at playing squash, so unfortunately, most of the time I can't even satisfy my ego by beating them, despite my being by far the youngest player there. Just to give the reader a bit of a background story, I played squash recreationally for a while, initially as a substitute for football (which I was getting too old for), but my occasional opponents kept getting injured. And I mean — constantly. I played once against one of my friends. He got injured — and that was him out for nearly half a year. Another guy kept getting injured in various DIY accidents. And so, to cut a long story short, I decided to join a proper club. I asked some of the guys who played at this fancy sports centre, and they let me play with them for a while, to see if I would fit in. As it turned out, I wasn't half as bad as I thought, and after a few sessions their captain extended an invitation to me to join on a permanent basis. I duly accepted. I think, secretly, they were ecstatic, since I considerably brought down the average age of their gang. More recently, I've even been granted access to the team's WhatsApp chat, which is another sign of being accepted into the hood. Initially, I thought this was a great thing, and I tried to comment and take part in the banter. But after a while, having seen the things my fellow teammates were writing about, I decided it would be wise to refrain from commenting, because my instinct would be to write things like "What a bunch of wusses you guys are." It goes without saying this probably wouldn't have gone down well. A conversation would go something like this:

Captain: Hello men, we're one player short for the first team, and need somebody from the second team to help out.

Mr X: Oh, I can't because I'm still recovering from my bad elbow, which has been bothering me for weeks now.

Mr Y: Oh, no, you poor thing, well, hope you get better soon.

Mr Z: Ditto, get well soon Mr X. Unfortunately, I can't either, because I have had a cold for quite some time, and it's been niggling for weeks.

Mr R: Oh no, Mr Z, you poor thing! Hope you get

better soon, drink plenty of herbal tea and keep yourself warm.

Can you imagine a conversation like that in a rugby team's dressing room?! Best case scenarios, if you started complaining about your cuts and bruises, you'd probably get a slap in the face. And that's exactly how I feel. But, obviously, if I started writing comments like "Shut up, you big loser!" or "Stop whining, you toss-pot," I'd have to look for another club pretty soon.

When you get these 'wusses' onto the squash court, however, things are completely different. They are extremely competitive and try to win every point, no matter what the score is. At first I was a bit stunned. A year ago, I wasn't on a par with even their weakest player — and he is a 74-year-old grandpa. Playing a game against their top players meant getting a regular beating of 11-1, 11-2, 11-0. It was at this point that I became aware of yet another cultural difference. Apparently there is no such thing as 'just having a game' for the sake of 'laugh', or to just enjoy playing against your opponent. Nope! Every game is taken very seriously and your opponent will try to win every point, irrespective of whether they are leading 10-0, which, I suppose, is not a bad thing if you have a competitive nature, which I do.

Before I go on a rant about German TV and how

German TV: *Tatort*

much I despise it, I have to take a moment to pay homage to German cinema and the important role it has played in the history of film-making. Before World War II, the arts and music scene was thriving in the Weimar Republic, and German filmmakers were at the forefront of the cinematic zeitgeist.

This creative Molotov cocktail produced directorial heavyweights like Fritz Lang, whose most notable cult films *Metropolis* (1927) and *M: Eine Stadt sucht einen Mörder* (A City is Looking for a Killer) have served as iconic hallmarks for future filmmakers all over the globe. So, yes, job well done, Germany.

As someone who is on the inside of the business — an avid film composer — the subject of film and music, and particularly the putting-together of moving images and sound, is one close to my heart. Having studied music and later a Master's in Music for the Screen, I consider myself knowledgeable on the subject. Since the eighties, growing up in four different countries, I've seen a lot of television in my lifetime. As a child, I was accustomed to Russian (or Soviet, at that time) TV; later I was exposed to Scandinavian and British television, and even later — and not by choice, I must say — I came across German TV in its purest form. So, I feel pretty well-put to state, definitively, that German TV is awful. Before I even begin my scornful fountain of projectile vomit in reference to

German TV, I will acknowledge that there will be a fair share of people who will vehemently deny my criticisms, shake their heads in disbelief, and dismiss my comments as some form of 'Anti-Germanisms'. But, naturally, we can ignore these nay-sayers. As a disclaimer, I have to clarify that, when referring to German TV, I am primarily talking about the terrestrial channels, and not the recent original Netflix and Sky masterpieces such as *Dark* and *Babylon Berlin,* for which I am full of praise.

So what exactly is my 'beef' with German TV, you may ask? Well, to put it in a nutshell — everything, really. From the diabolical storylines, atrocious pantomime-like acting, ancient camera and editing techniques that stink of the seventies, grotesque use of musical cues and worst of all — the never-ending dialogue. If I were to encompass all of these shortcomings in one show, then they would perfectly fit one label: Tatort. This crime detective series is a bit of an institution in Germany. If you ever ask a German person what they are doing on a Sunday between 8pm and 9pm, you will undoubtedly hear them say, "I'm watching Tatort." If you have any sense, you should follow up with a cheeky question: "Why?" But that will not increase your chance of making friends in Germany, I can assure you of that. *Tatort* has been around since the seventies — making it the longest-running German TV drama ever — and the people making it, evidently, are still the same ones that did it back then. Just see the opening credits for proof.

The interesting part is that pretty much every major city in Germany can boast an episode that was filmed in that city — because Tatort is jointly produced by regional stations all across Germany, who each contribute a few episodes per year. So, if you're from Munich, you can look forward to the episode dedicated to Munich and its police team. The same goes for Leipzig, Hamburg, Berlin and so forth. So part of the fun, I presume, is to see if you can recognise any of the locations where the episode was filmed. Perhaps that is the point, and instead, I've been banging on about cinematography, craftsmanship, creativity, and all that nonsense instead. But let's set the 'Where's Wally' location finder fun aside for a minute and look at the actual film-making factor. The last episode I actually watched was purely for research purposes for this book, and that is an hour of my life I'll never get back. To elucidate all of my criticisms of German TV, I've taken a scene from the episode, which lasts about five minutes. Indeed, if I wanted to point out the shortcomings of the entire episode, I would need to write an extra book.

And thus, Scene X: a police van is transporting a high security prisoner from one location to another. All of a sudden, when travelling through a dodgy woodland area, the prisoner gets the urge to go for a pee and asks the police officers to stop the van. Initially, they refuse, but the prisoner is very persistent and exclaims, "I need to go!" This appears to be enough to convince the highly trained special ops officers, so they wave to the driver to stop the bus, as you do. At this point the prisoner insults one of the police officers, the one who is obviously an extra, and doesn't have any dialogue. His reaction is similar to one you might see at a panto, when somebody says, "Oh look!" and points in a different direction. He has obviously been instructed by the producer to look 'angry'. The only problem is, they forgot to teach him how to act — or in this case, rather, how not to act. What ensues makes even less sense, even in a David Lynch-esque bizarre world of logic. A car pulls up on the horizon, and then turns into a side road. One of the officers (the main character) goes to investigate — again, as you do — and the camera follows him. While he is out of sight, he hears gunshots. The car turns out to be a false alarm, so he runs up to the corner of the alley, pulls out his gun, and points it towards the police van, which is about one hundred metres away. At this point a vein on my forehead began to twitch. My eyelids began to flicker in a kind of a nervous dismay. The officer sees the van pulling off and accelerating past him, with the prisoner presumably in it, driven by one of the coppers, who obviously was not a cop at all. The good cop aims at the speeding van in the distance and fires several shots, as we have seen in many scenes in the seventies gangster movies. Two other officers are dead, lying on the ground next to the spot where the van had been parked.

End scene.

> **Good to know:**
>
> *Essentially, there are two state broadcasters in Germany that you need to be aware of: ARD and ZDF. The ARD, which stands for Arbeitsgemeinschaft der öffentlich-rechtlichen Rundfunkanstalten der Bundesrepublik Deutschland, (the Union of the State Broadcaster of the German Federal Republic), also known as Das Erste, is a no-frills, current affairs type of broadcaster, where you'll mostly see very serious and stiff faces, whose presenters are dressed — or so it appears — for Sunday mass. Their demeanour is always formal and contained, always beginning their reportage with a formal "Guten Tag". The latter, ZDF, has a less cryptic acronym that stands for Zweites Deutsches Fernsehen (Second German Television), and is more focused on entertainment. Here, for example, you will find the German version of The Daily Show — called TV Total, presented by a guy called Stefan Raab, who, even by British standards, can be quite entertaining at times.*

Whether or not you decide to spend any of your time watching German terrestrial channels is up to you. However, irrespective of the fact, every household in Germany has to pay a TV licence fee of approximately two hundred euros per year. Depending on how much you love or despise German television and radio, this fact can add to your level of disgruntlement or joy.

The German sauna

Picture yourself in the middle of a room, that's only slightly bigger than a spare room in a moderately sized semi-detached house in an average suburb. Now, imagine it filled with people, completely naked, panting and sweating, sitting on neatly folded towels, meticulously making sure that no part of their body is touching the wooden bench. Surprisingly enough, they don't make any attempt to use any part of the towel to cover their private parts (which should be anyone's natural instinct). The temperature on the thermometer shows ninety degrees. The place is packed. The clock strikes seven pm, and without any delay a man in his twenties enters the room wearing a sleek towel wrapped around his waist, holding a wooden jug filled with what appears to be water. Politely, he greets everyone in the room, as a matter of routine, in exactly the same fashion that he's done countless times before. He doesn't add any extra words. He doesn't joke or smile at anyone. He simply follows the same procedure.

"Good evening ladies and gentlemen. Welcome to this *Aufguss*. This *Aufguss* consists of lemongrass essence and scents of pine needles. We will have three rounds in total. You can leave the room at any point of your choosing."

His voice and actions seem so banal (considering the setting) that you might think he's a train manager announcing the next arrival at Euston Station. He then carefully pours the contents of the jug on the open stove and slowly works the room, waving his towel above the head at even intervals to spread the ensuing heat wave. This has an astonishing effect on the people in the room. Without warning, some begin to pant, exalt loudly with an ecstatic *"Ja!"*, rub their sweaty bodies all over, and make other strange noises which can only be associated with cataclysmic orgasms, the likes of which are best kept secret within the confinement of one's own four walls. Despite the surreal setting I've just described to you, this 'ritual' has a strict order to which everyone adheres. The procedure lasts approximately ten minutes, after which the man politely thanks everyone and exits the sauna.

Once he leaves, other people start exiting the room — in an orderly fashion — which goes without saying.

For any foreigner experiencing this for the first time, it's a massive shock to the system that (if one's not careful) could cause a mild cardiac arrest. But, for any citizen of the Bundesrepublik, this event is as normal as peeling potatoes, and is an intrinsic part of the sauna etiquette that has been around for as long as anyone remembers. If you want to fit in with the Germans — and if you're reading the book I'm presuming you do — then it's essential to get to know the following rules of sauna going.

- Always bring two large towels — one to sit on, and one to wipe yourself clean after showering, or in case your other towel isn't large enough for you to put your feet on. N.B. If you're really aiming to impress your German colleagues, then wear a white robe.
- Make sure you bring flip flops, as walking barefoot is frowned upon.
- Do not try to cover your genitals whilst walking around the sauna premises. The towels should either hang on your shoulder, or be carried in your hand.
- Before entering the sauna, make sure you read the *'Sauna Regeln'*, which are usually posted at every entrance.
- If you want to spot people from East Germany, out of sheer interest, look at the size of their towels and the type of swimwear they have. The smaller the towel, the greater the likelihood of them being from

the East. The same goes for the swimming trunks. So, somebody wearing leopard skin speedos and carrying a tiny towel — unmistakably from the East.

- Do not strike up conversations with strangers. Mind your own business.
- Keep your gaze firmly at eye level.

Having lived in Germany for over fifteen years, I still haven't been able to fully grasp this superimposed normality. It is the only place in the world that I can think of where you get looks of disapproval if you commit the capital sin of wearing a bathing suit. It might not stop there, as those feeling particularly concerned might even take it upon themselves to tell you off for doing so, stopping just short of ripping your trunks right off. At the very least, you'll feel completely ostracised and 'naked', if you will excuse the pun.

If this is all too much for you, then the only advice I can give you is to avoid the place altogether and never set foot inside. You can instead dedicate your leisure time towards the arts, literature, culture, and theatre — although, as you will soon find out, you might not be able to escape the nudity factor entirely.

Culture doesn't just refer to how people think and

Chapter 5

Arts, Culture, History & Religion: In a nutshell

interact. According to Cristina De Rossi, an anthropologist at Barnet and Southgate College in London, "Culture also means refined intellectual, artistic and creative achievement, for example as in cultural knowledge, or a cultured person." Indeed, Germany is a cultural mecca; no matter whether you're into history, architecture, music, poetry, philosophy or literature, Germany has something to offer everyone. This is one of the reasons why Germans are (inwardly) so proud of their country and their language. Every year, tourists from all over the world flock to the *Bundesrepublik*, particularly during the summer months. The capital city of Berlin, for instance, attracts over 135 million people each year. With its unique status as the former colossus that was once divided into East and West, Berlin remains one of the most fascinating cities in the world.

Germans have made tremendous contributions to Europe's great stock of 'arts and culture'. Known for being a nation of thinkers, Germans pride themselves on their impressive track record in music, literature, architecture, theatre, poetry, philosophy, and even religion. Indeed, the magnitude of cultural influence Germany has had on European heritage is overwhelming. The list of Germany's claims to fame is very impressive indeed. For example, consider the sheer number of musical heavyweights that have emerged from German-speaking countries: Johann Sebastian Bach, Wolfgang Amadeus Mozart, Ludwig van Beethoven, Johannes Brahms, Richard Wagner and Gustav Mahler, to name a few. When it comes to literature,

Germany can boast titans like Goethe, Schiller, Mann, Heine and Kafka; while German characters like Martin Luther played a pivotal role in the most important religious transformation in the history of Christianity. Fast forward a few centuries, and there's Brecht, overhauling the theatre scene with his radical dramaturgical ideas, while Kant and Nietzsche's polarised thinking forever changed how we approach philosophy. Even modern psychology has got a German fingerprint on it thanks to Sigmund Freud. And even taking all of that into account, we've barely scratched the surface. Let's dive a little deeper.

Don't mention the war

One of the party tricks my American friend Champlin used to do at house parties — back in the days when I actually went to parties — was to take the cellophane packaging from an empty cigarette packet, put it to his mouth, and recite sentences taken from *Third Reich* propaganda speeches. By placing the cellophane over his mouth, he could uncannily emulate the sound of a crackling radio, the kind that were used in the 1920s. I distinctly remember the reaction it got: all of the expats were rolling on the floor, clutching their stomachs. However, anyone who was German was dismayed, almost in shock at the audacity of the trick.

Before I came to Germany, I already had a preconception of what its people were like, based upon cliché sayings taken from a cult British comedy troupe — *Monty Python* — and the countless jokes I heard from my stepdad when I was growing up in the UK. Most jokes poke fun at the Germans for being completely devoid of humour, stiff in appearance and manners, and generally just really strange people that no one knows how to behave around.

Up to this day, World War II, The Third Reich, Nazism and concentration camps remain difficult topics for German people to talk about. If you dare raise it in a social context, you will most likely make the people around you feel uneasy. And God forbid you crack a joke about it — within seconds you will descend into a dark oblivion that is called 'no friends', and no one will want to talk to you.

A stark reminder of how seriously the people and the state take this notion is the fact that you can still get arrested for shouting *"Heil Hitler"* in public in Germany, or for doing a Hitler salute. Quite recently, I read a story about some Chinese tourists getting in trouble for doing just that in Berlin. To an outsider, this seems a little excessive, considering the fact that seventy-five years have elapsed since the end of the Third Reich and the gruesome atrocities that were committed under Hitler. And yet, you don't see Americans (North Americans, that is) telling foreigners off for cracking jokes about Native Americans, or the English looking sternly at anyone telling jokes about the Pakistanis. But this is off-topic. The fact of the matter is that several generations have passed since the end of World War II, but many would say that in Germany the present generation still feel this burden on their shoulders.

If you ask any teenager in the latter stages of their high school education about the field trips they have done with their class, you can be certain that they will have visited one of the concentration camps. At school, every history curriculum will have the *Third Reich* listed as a compulsory topic from as early as the seventh grade. Countless documentaries are shown on terrestrial channels about Nazism, World War II and the Holocaust. And thus, Germany does not shy away from its difficult past; on the contrary, it drills it into its citizens from a young age. One of my historian friends refers to this phenomenon as collective guilt. As he puts it, this is ingrained into German society. It gets attached to every person from the moment they are born as a German citizen, like a strand of DNA that is passed on to you from your ancestors, and stays with you until you perish. It is the German person's constant burden to try to atone for the crimes of their forebears. Equally, it is considered their duty to pass this burden onto the next generation. In the United States, patriotism comes as standard. In fact, being *unpatriotic* amounts to being an *enemy of the people*. In Germany, it is exactly the reverse. Patriotism has been added to the list of sins.

Germans love their country, and yet, they are not allowed to openly express this. This is in stark contrast to every other country in the world. It might sound strange to anyone who is not from Germany, but to most people who were born here, being *patriotic* is akin to being a right-wing neo-Nazi. This has been a hotly-debated topic for a very long time. One of the most bizarre events I've witnessed in my time in Germany was during the World Cup of 2006, which was hosted by the federal republic. An article appeared in a German newspaper, which prompted a huge debate that engulfed the whole country. That debate was about putting up German flags. A lot of people obviously wanted to show their support for the national team, and had bought flags to hang outside of their properties. Somehow, these people were accused of being neo-Nazis, right-wing yobs, and anti-Semites.

It is perhaps unsurprising, given Germany's history, that the flag — or any other display of overt nationalism — has become such a thorny subject. But the more Germany continues to unflinchingly face up to its difficult past — and attempt to atone for it — with countless museums, memorials and remembrance days, the louder some voices on the fringes are growing, arguing that enough is enough and that Germany can't simply feel guilty forever. One far-right politician memorably referred to the Holocaust memorial in Berlin as a 'monument of shame' in the heart of the capital. His words — in breaking with the country's postwar consensus to remember and atone for Nazi crimes — caused an outpouring of condemnation at the time, but it is difficult to imagine any other country in the world subjecting itself to such a continuous display of guilt and shame. Take Berlin as an example. If you happen to be in the German capital around 9th May — the day officially celebrated as the end of World War II — you will witness a highly peculiar spectacle: cars driving the streets with Russian flags in their windows; loud, nationalist victory songs in Russian playing from various apartments; an obligatory article in *Der Spiegel* and other news outlets remembering the victims of the Nazi regime and the peril it brought upon the world of our great-grandparents, whilst also using it as a stark reminder to all future generations not to repeat the same mistakes. Could you imagine anything like this done anywhere else in the world? For example, imagine German citizens celebrating the collapse of communism and the fall of the Berlin Wall on 9th November in the Russian capital. Or perhaps Indians celebrating the end of colonial British rule in London, while newspapers publish scores of stories about the atrocities committed by the British Empire. Or Algerians riding through the streets of Paris celebrating their independence from the French, as a monument to the natives slaughtered during the Algerian Revolution is erected next to the *Arc de Triomphe*. The answer is no. Anyone attempting to do anything of the sort would be lynched by a mob of angry patriots. But not in Germany, where the past must be constantly faced up to, and atoned for.

It is thus not surprising that one of the worst things you can accuse a German of — on a par with not being punctual, not paying their taxes, and crossing the road on red — is patriotism. Slogans like "proud to be British", which are encouraged in the UK, are taboo in Germany. *Proud to be German* would instantly have a negative connotation, although it can be difficult for non-Germans to really see why that is. Perhaps it's the double-decker bus that's missing. Whatever the case may be, you have been warned: don't do Nazi jokes in any shape or form, or else risk being ostracised from German social circles.

Humour & Funny Germans

"Same procedure as every year."

On the New Year's Eve of 2002, I remember sitting together with my flatmates in our shared apartment in Hamburg-Altona — my first ever New Year in Germany — watching the festive television broadcasts. I was flicking aimlessly through the channels, when our only German flatmate yelled, "Leave it here!" He had obviously spotted something he wanted to watch, so I went back to the previous channel. It was an 18-minute long, black-and-white two-hander sketch about a woman's ninetieth birthday, and her butler, who gets progressively more drunk as the evening develops. Up to that day, I had never heard of it, so imagine my surprise when my flatmate told me that this 1963 relic, called Dinner for One, actually originated in the UK. Despite remaining almost completely unknown in its home country, it has since acquired a cult following in Germany and, as it turns out, forms the basis of their understanding of what the British find *funny*. It is aired on almost every single German terrestrial channel in the lead-up to New Year's Eve — in some instances more than once — presumably to accommodate its huge popularity. In contrast, since its release, it has only been shown once in the UK.

Universally, there are many physical attributes that make us identify with other human beings. We all — or at least most of us — have two legs, one head, two ears, two arms, fingers on our hands, and so on and so forth. The ability to speak the same language is another one. But for the sake of this book, I'm referring to one thing in particular: our ability to laugh. Be it a hearty genuine one, a little snigger at a clever remark, or even laughing out of desperation (it's the standard British recourse when we feel embarrassed). It doesn't matter. What does matter is the bond created when two or more people laugh together in the same place, at the same moment, and for the same reason. Apart from the chemical reactions, a simultaneous laugh creates a subliminal connection. No doubt the topic deserves a book of its own, and many have been written — I'm sure.

For somebody from an Anglo-Saxon or an Anglo-American culture in particular, humour is not just something that happens on the periphery. For the most part, humour is essential to our lives. Without this quality, our days would be filled with boring routine tasks, overly repetitive, dull and a bit meaningless. If you're not from a country where English is a native language, you might think that last remark was a bit dramatic. But believe 'you me', it is not an exaggeration. And if you have doubts about my *scholarly* expertise in Anglo-Saxon culture (and if you know anything about me as the author of this book — you probably should), then ask a true *Brit* and they will concur; I am absolutely sure of that.

With that in mind, it is easy to draw a line between the British sense of humour, i.e. the one where jokes are part of everyday life, and the German equivalent. The big difference: in Germany, humour and jokes have a special place and time, but they are not essential to one's existence. Inventive uses of language, such as irony, sarcasm and witticisms, would go straight over a German person's head, not because they do not exist in the German language – they do — but primarily due to the fact that your use of those terms will not follow the set rules as to application, timing and, most importantly of all, place. So, my advice: if you do tell a joke, make sure to immediately follow it up with the words "that was a joke". The alternative is to forget humour altogether, as depressing as that may sound, at least until you've mastered all the nuances and intricacies of German language and culture.

Are Germans funny? As I've already mentioned, the most common thing said about the Germans is that they lack a sense of humour, that they're too serious, and that they don't get jokes at all. An element of truth, or simply a cultural thing? Let's take a deeper look.

At a time when the Brits were being educated by John Cleese, Graham Chapman and Rowan Atkinson — the former responsible for *Monty Python, Life of Brian and The Holy Grail* in the seventies, and the latter for the world-renowned satirical character of *Mr. Bean* — in Germany, a certain comedian was enthralling audiences with his short sketches. His name was Bernhard-Viktor Christoph-Carl von Bülow (1923-2011), better known by his stage name Loriot. His cartoon drawings were made into TV sketches and became an overnight hit. Essentially a satire depicting different German stereotypes, Loriot is written with witty dialogue, coated in good old family TV charm, suitable for all ages. It's a bit like Mr Bean, but with dialogue. One of his famous sketches is called *Die Ente bleibt draussen* (The Duck Must Remain Outside), in which two middle-aged men both find themselves sharing a bath, arguing over whether a rubber duck should remain in the tub. But perhaps the most famous sketch of all is *Das Bild hängt schief* (The Picture is Askew), in which a man tries to correct a wonky picture frame in a public waiting room. He fails in his mission, and instead manages to turn the whole room upside down. *Loriot* is charming, inoffensive, easily digestible, and 100 percent German.

The complete antithesis to *Loriot*, showing the 'dark side of the moon', is a German comedian called Helge Schneider. Born in 1955 in North Rhine-Westphalia, Schneider, whilst also an accomplished jazz musician, multi-instrumentalist and film director, is best known for his absurd songs like *Katzeklo* (Cat Toilet), and his self-directed films *Texas* (1993), *00 Schneider* (1994) and *Jazz Club* (2004). Indeed, Schneider's combined discography has more than twenty-four releases spanning three decades. He also has eight films to his name. As such, anyone who dismisses German humour as either underdeveloped, or as simply not funny, obviously hasn't seen any of Helge's movies. The guy is pure genius and his films encompass the most sophisticated forms of *'Schwarzes Humor'* (black humour): a combination of sarcasm, self-mockery, pseudo-improv, and even elements of Dadaism, an *Avant Garde* movement which sprang to life at the beginning of the twentieth century.

Comedians like Schneider might epitomise the complexity and the extent of German humour, and thus show how much it has developed since the sixties and seventies, but the question of why the British do not consider German humour 'funny' isn't difficult to understand. Aside from the obvious cultural and linguistic differences, the other important element is the absence of self-mockery from what is considered 'being funny' in Germany. Contrary to the British, Germans do not like to mock themselves, neither in private, nor in public. A joke at your own expense is never funny, but rather humiliating and degrading. Whereas in many countries mocking oneself is seen as an indication of strong character and personal strength — i.e. someone who is confident enough to put themself in the spotlight and allow others a laugh at their expense — in Germany, this concept is completely alien. Trying to make fun of yourself in front of a German will only cause confusion and will make you, as the source of it all, feel misunderstood, and ostracised from the group. Even worse, you might even cause further embarrassment to your German friends — a classic case of *Fremdschämen.*

Contrary to popular belief, however, Germans can be very sarcastic. The difference is, their sarcasm is extremely dry. In other words, there is no indication that someone is being sarcastic — none whatsoever. There is no traceable change in their intonation, timbre, or enunciation that gives the reader a clue. The only way to be sure would be to counter it with an equally sarcastic response, and see if they react to it. Only then would you be able to decipher the true nature of their remark. A common bonding tool the Brits use is to lightly poke fun at the other person — a true sign that you feel comfortable with each other. It shows to the person on the receiving end that your guard has been let down, and that you can speak your mind freely and candidly. To a certain extent, the Germans do the same thing. However, the nature of their sarcasm is much stealthier, virtually untraceable, and is done less in favour of bonding, and more in order to disguise their true comment, so that they can't be accused of being *mean* — an insurance policy of sorts.

Coming back to our *Dinner for One* analogy, let's say that it is easy to get things wrong about somebody else's sense of humour, particularly if you lack the cultural and linguistic knowledge required to fully comprehend it as an outsider. Granted, to your dismay, the Germans will most likely 'leave you hanging' when you expect to be high-fived after your witty comments, or praised when using a hefty dose of self-mockery. Despite that, I urge you not to be hasty in branding the whole nation as 'having no sense of humour'. To my great personal relief, I have found *Dinner for One* getting progressively better every year: a direct correlation to the amount of alcohol I drink while watching it. Last year, I managed to watch all four repeats on ARD. Sadly though, I cannot recall a thing after that, and only remember waking up with a hangover the morning after.

Popular music

For the sake of this chapter, I'm going to put all the great German classical composers to one side, leaving the reader with the choice of exploring all the Mozarts, Beethovens, Schuberts and Brahmses at their leisure, and instead, I'm going to focus on the popular music tradition in Germany, which is perhaps less known to the outsider, and thus more interesting to read about — or so you might think.

A little background: Having myself been a full-blooded musician prior to taking up full-time teaching, the topic of music is a particularly sensitive one for me, and in a way, particularly painful to write about. Thinking about German music often causes various gastric reactions and other unpleasant sensations in my body. And this is not because German popular music is *bad* per se — it's not. I mean, it's no worse than any of the other commercial garbage aimed at twelve-to-sixteen-year-olds that we hear these days, picked out by machine algorithms that the labels have spent a fortune on. No, this is not the main reason.

But to say that Germany does not have a rich music tradition would be grossly incorrect. In fact — it does — based on its history and its own unique taste. For example, the 1920s Berlin was a thriving hub for Cabaret and small-stage theatre that bore witness to the likes of the *Comedian Harmonists* (a male acapella group), *Chansonieres* such as Marlene Dietrich, and spoken theatre, to name but a few elements. To this day, these forms of expression are very much in vogue, and retain a coveted place in German cultural establishments, and in the hearts of German people.

English language aside, let's have a look at the chronology of German music scene.

After World War II, there wasn't much going on, for obvious reasons. However, with the division of East and West came an outpouring of creative energy, as German bands all subtly and not-so-subtly rebelled against the communist state. For example, the emergence of mainstream rock 'n' roll in the fifties and punk rock in the sixties and seventies were mirrored by similar developments in Germany. Nobody could escape the Presleys, the Beatles, the Dylans and the Stones, and so German musicians embraced the rebel spirit with open arms — although, naturally, they did it in their own language. Then came the happy-go-lucky seventies and eighties with their frizzy hairdos, colourful outfits, and snazzy attitudes to match. At the same time, groundbreaking, experimental electronic music from the likes of Kraftwerk was emerging from the musty basements of Berlin and Düsseldorf. This era also saw bands like Nena and *Modern Talking* taking centre stage with their cheeky synthy-pop music. The emergence of German hip hop in the nineties paved the way for a different kind of expression. The absence of *singing* and the emergence of rap suited the German language very well, and it quickly became very popular among German teenagers, who were desperately searching for a voice that was different to the previous generation. Bands like Die Fantastische Vier, Fettes Brot and Jan Delay all pay homage to this genre and reflect the youth culture of the time.

Back to the topic of English language: Throughout the history of German pop, very few bands have made hits in English, and there is a very good reason for that. Have you ever noticed that the moment Germans switch from their native language and begin to sing songs in English, things start to go horribly wrong? I'm not talking about the chart artists, but rather in the entertainment industry: cover bands, musical singers, hotel musicians, that sort of thing. In fact, I've lost count the amount of times my ears have had to endure listening to ghastly pronunciation of popular hits like *Summer of 69* by Brian Adams, which roughly sounded like this: "PLAID IT 'TILL MAI FINGERZ BLED, WOZ A SAMMA OF ZIX-TI NEIN!"; or cringing to an unbearable rendition of Marvin Gaye's *Sunny*, which went like this: "SANNI, YESTERDEI MAI LAIF WOZ FILD WIZ REIN." The pain I suffered got instantly worse when I saw the German audience were seemingly impressed, and not at all bothered by the pronunciation. This was confirmed by them determinedly clapping on beats one and three (as German audiences do, in stark contrast to the rest of the world, where people clap on two and four). As an afterthought, doing something quite badly to an audience that does not know the difference between what's good or bad seems to work too — Germany being the case in point, so I guess I've just defeated my own argument with my own *counterargument*. In the end, why should a nation like Germany, with a population of over eighty million and a rich language tradition, care about a few 'frowning' expats (as I write this last sentence, a piece of me is dying inside).

A list of all the successful German artists and bands that sang in English and enjoyed international success in the past fifty years:

- Modern Talking — whose iconic singer Dieter Bohlen — akin to Simon Cowell in the English-speaking world — is now on the jury panel for *Deutschland sucht den Superstar*.
- The Scorpions — the iconic rock band of the eighties and nineties, whose timeless power ballads — par-

ticularly the song *Winds of Change* — still appear on regular radio playlists.

- Nena — another iconic singer whose *99 Red Balloons* — a song about the fall of the Berlin Wall — engraved her initials into German musical folklore.
- Alphaville — probably the only German band that made it into the big eighties power-ballad legacy, with its cult hits such as *Forever Young*, and *Big in Japan*.
- Fury in the Slaughterhouse — a band with a funny name, whom I only know based on their one hit, *Time to Wonder.*
- *Rammstein* — these prog-rock heavy hitters are a household name in Germany and abroad too, although technically they mostly sing in German, save maybe a couple of songs like 'TE QUIERO PUTA', which is in Spanish anyway.

Aside from that there are a few other bands that have enjoyed international success to various degrees. These include: Cascada, Fools Garden, Falco, Kraftwerk, Lou Bega and Tokio Hotel.

You might have noticed that I left a certain Hans Zimmer out of the equation. This is partly due to the fact that he writes instrumental film music, and partly due to the fact that he himself can hardly speak his native German tongue any longer. He is virtually American.

Schlager Schlager

Every nation has its own music genre which epitomises the heart and soul of its citizens. In Germany this is *Schlager*. Describing *Schlager* as a foreigner is not easy, but if you asked any German what they associate with this particular genre of music, they will undoubtedly mention wild parties, ridiculous outfits, lots of alcohol, and of course the *Schlagermove*, pronounced as 'SchlagerMOVE'. This is a term coined for a Schlager festival which originated in 1997 in Hamburg. After its inauguration, it quickly gained popularity all over Germany and subsequently other cities like Hannover, Essen and Dortmund started hosting their own versions of *Schlagermove*, but under the slightly different name of *Schlager-Parade*. The biggest modern *Schlager* icon in Germany is Helene Fischer, whose music people either love or hate, depending on whether they have a taste for *music* or not. The songs usually consist of catchy disco tunes with generic lyrics about the usual topic of love, carefully created in a music lab by at least eight producers, to be consumed by the masses *en masse*. And, of course, it works! Thus, if you love *Schlager*, you'll love Helene Fischer. It's a simple formula. Over the years, Fischer has evolved from a typical young poster girl — she is slim and blonde, with perfect hair and blue eyes — into a thirty-something-working-mum type of persona. She can sing and move on the stage, and as long as the stage lights are on and the wind machine is working, German audiences will continue to adore her.

Incidentally, there are two different types of *Schlager* in Germany: there is *old Schlager*, which is sung in concert halls, with its charming and beautifully crafted melodies, supported by lush orchestras; and then there is *modern Schlager,* the blow-your-brains (and eardrums) type of music, composed around a heavy disco beat. This new type of *Schlager* is often played at the so-called *Apreski* clubs and bars on the snowy pistes of Austria, Switzerland and Italy.

Musicals

Musicals are very popular in Germany, and prior to the COVID-19 pandemic which brought pretty much every theatre in the country to its knees, musical theatre has always thrived in big German cities. The success of *The Lion King*, which is the longest-performing musical in Germany, deserves a mention. Similarly, *The Phantom of the Opera* has been seen by literally millions of Germans, and it is still one of the most popular musicals to date. For me, and I emphasise the word *me*, the only problem with German musicals — or should I say with English musicals translated into German — is that they are all in *bloody German*. You might have noticed that the German language is not the softest or the most romantic of languages. And so you might entertain the thought of giving *das Phantom der Oper* a go, since it's one of the more linguistically brutal and operatic musicals out there; you might even enjoy der *König der Löwen* (The Lion King), primarily because the music is so amazing, although you will probably chuckle at the fact that most singers in it are not German; but you will definitely cringe during the German rendition of the inexorably 'British' *Mary Poppins* when you hear the extra notes and awkward squeezes needed to fit in all of the syllables of the German translation. The famous line "Just a spoonful of sugar helps the medicine go down" becomes *"Gerade hilft ein Löffel Zucker der Medizin hinunterzugehen"*, and that's when you begin to wish that a light fixture would accidentally drop on the female protagonist, bringing both her misery and your own to a swift and well-deserved end.

Theatre & Obsession with nudity

In 2004 I was a member of a jazz choir at the Music Conservatoire in Hamburg — an esteemed higher education institution – one that prides itself on producing some of the best musicians in Germany. Anyway, I'll spare you the back story and cut to the chase. One of the guys in the choir invited me to a theatre production that they were putting on and told me it would be *worthwhile*. Within a week I had organised tickets for myself and a few of my friends who were into arts and *culture*, that sort of thing. I managed to get really good seats, right in the front row, and was very chuffed with myself for managing such a feat. I was really looking forward to immersing myself in German culture. About an hour and a half into the production, the main protagonist began undressing himself during a monologue, facing the audience. One item at a time, he was taking his kit off in front of a packed theatre. By the time he only had his underpants left, I distinctly remember thinking, 'surely not?' — a doubt which was quickly dispelled when he emphatically took them off. Unfortunately, there was no time for the shock to settle in, because in the seconds that followed, the whole cast repeated the action and followed suit — until everyone on stage was stark naked. Fifteen years later, and countless hours spent in front of a psychologist, I still haven't fully gotten over the ordeal. Okay, that last sentence was said in jest, but you get the idea — it was a bloody traumatic experience! Unsurprisingly, I cannot for the life of me remember the title of the play, nor can I remember a single line from it, and even more worryingly, the names of the people I went with. Important lesson for the theatre-goers in Germany: getting better seats with a better view does not always work in your favour.

Indeed, the somewhat casual attitude towards nakedness in Germany extends beyond FKK *(Freiköperkultur)* and into theatre houses. For some reason, German theatre directors seem to have an obsession with making their actors and actresses take their kit off on stage, and this happens more often than you might think. So much so that a whole book has been dedicated to this matter alone. *One Hundred Years of Nakedness in German Performance* (1988) is a title by Karl Toepfer. In it, he argues that exposing one's naked body onstage is a way of elevating *realism* to a new level. Another suggestion is that the act of displaying nakedness and the act of observing nakedness together form a powerful set of political values. Whatever the case may be, you might want to think twice before taking your whole family on a cultural day out to the theatre in the *Bundesrepublik* — take my word for it.

Important Germans:

Bertolt Brecht (1898-1956)

There is a great tradition of theatre in Germany, which is partly due to the rich history of spoken theatre in the postwar era. Anyone who has ever studied theatre will inevitably have heard of Bertolt Brecht (1898-1956). Brecht was considered the founder of *epic theatre,* which went against the tradition of Greek Tragedy, i.e. evoking emotions and catharsis, in favour of the so-called sachlich (matter of fact) state of mind. To put it in layman's words, Brecht's plays were about the action, rather than epitomising action itself. His most notable play — *The Threepenny Opera* (1931) — was a play with musical numbers, with songs written by his long-standing collaborator Kurz Weil, perhaps best remembered for the song *Mack the Knife*, which features in the play. Brecht also pioneered the so-called *Verfremdungseffekt* (the alienation effect), which demanded actors be aware of the fact that they are *de facto* — acting. Actors were also often required to break the *fourth wall*, i.e. address the audience in the theatre directly, thereby breaking the sacred tradition of his predecessors and contemporaries alike, e.g. Konstantin Stanislavski (1863-1938).

German literature

If you've ever received any kind of a greetings card from an older German person, be it a birthday, Christmas, or an anniversary, you might notice that these often contain different types of poetry, limericks, or even parables. This, as I'm sure you'll agree, requires a lot more effort than simply writing "MERRY CHRISTMAS.... from JOHN" in a ten-pack of Christmas cards, purchased in ALDI during the January sales. At times I've been moved by the effort they've gone to, and in other cases, even slightly annoyed — mostly because I've realised that a reply of "Merry CHRIMBO, cheers, FADI" wouldn't be sufficient, and even a bit *rude.*

To fully understand the tradition of such greetings, we need to look at Germany's colossal output of literature over the past few centuries: a country that has produced some of the greatest writers of all time. German influence is to this day omnipresent in all aspects of western thinking and philosophy. Granted, I cannot summarise all that Germany has done for literature in a few paragraphs; that would be like explaining the meaning of life with the number forty-two (a reference to the popular science fiction novel *The Hitchhiker's Guide to the Galaxy,* in case this one's lost on you). Nonetheless, I will list some of what Germans themselves consider the most important *oeuvres*. And what better way to do that, than delving into a secondary school German literature curriculum, courtesy of a friend who is a German teacher. Thanks, German teacher friend.

Important Germans:

Johann Wolfgang von Goethe (1749-1832)

This German figure will likely retain his status as the greatest German writer of all time for years to come. If you haven't heard of this author, you will at least have heard of the Goethe Institute, which is named after him. His most celebrated work, *Faust* (1790) is a two-part tragic play. In the first part of the play, the devil *Memphisto*, makes a bet with God: he says that he can tempt God's favourite human being (Faust), who is striving to learn everything that can be known, away from righteous pursuits. To summarise in one sentence — *Faust* is a play about an ambitious man who surrenders his moral integrity for a quick gain of power and success. As the storyline suggests, this book is not going to be a relaxing bed-time reading (Shakespeare's Macbeth springs to mind), but for anyone who is keen on extending their fountain of knowledge in the German classics, this is definitely the way forward.

Friedrich Schiller (1759-1805)

Another guy in a waistcoat, with a powdered face and a wig and considered one of German literary greats, is Friedrich Schiller (1759-1805). A contemporary and an acquaintance of von Goethe, Schiller is perhaps best known for his drama The Robbers *(Die Räuber)*. According to Wikipedia, 'The plot revolves around the conflict between two aristocratic brothers, Karl and Franz Moor. The charismatic but rebellious student Karl is deeply loved by his father. The younger brother, Franz, who appears as a cold, calculating villain, plots to wrest away Karl's inheritance. As the play unfolds, both Franz's motives and Karl's innocence and heroism are revealed to be complex.'.. 'Schiller raises many disturbing issues in the play. For instance, he questions the dividing lines between personal liberty and the law and probes the psychology of power, the nature of masculinity and the essential differences between good and evil. He strongly criticizes both the hypocrisies of class and religion and the economic inequities of German society. He also conducts a complicated inquiry into the nature of evil.' Indeed, moral integrity is a cornerstone of modern German society, so should you wish to get a better insight, feel free to breeze through the 118 pages of this play.

Heinrich Heine (1797-1856)

Heinrich Heine is another celebrated German poet, writer and literary critic. Best known for his lyrical texts, which were later used by composers such as Franz Schubert and Robert Schumann in their songs *(Lieder)*. His prose is distinguished for [to all my British friends] *satirical wit and irony.* He was a revisionist and his radical political views stirred a great deal of controversy at the time; his publications were banned by the authorities, inadvertently making him even more popular.

Franz Kafka (1883 - 1924)

If you're an avid film buff, and David Lynch means something to you, then you could say that Kafka was to German literary world what Lynch is to the cinematic world. Kafka was a bohemian novelist, whose writing encompasses elements of realism and the fantastic. His works typically feature isolated protagonists facing bizarre or surrealistic predicaments and incomprehensible socio-bureaucratic powers. It has been interpreted as exploring themes of alienation, existential anxiety, guilt, and absurdity. His best known works include *Die Verwandlung* (The Metamorphosis), *Der Process* (The Trial), and *Das Schloss* (The Castle). ar.

Max Rudolf Frisch (1911 – 1991)

Max Rudolf Frisch was a Swiss playwright and novelist. Frisch's works focused on problems of identity, individuality, responsibility, morality, and political commitment. The use of iron yis a significant feature of his post-war output. His most notable work, Andorra (1966), is a play based in a fictional place called *Andorra* (no relation to the actual country), which explores themes of cultural prejudice, whitewashing, and hypocrisy.

Hermann Karl Hesse (1877 – 1962)

Hermann Karl Hesse (1877 – 1962) was a German-born Swiss poet, novelist, and painter. His best-known works include *Demian, Steppenwolf, Siddhartha,* and *The Glass Bead Game,* each of which explores an individual's search for authenticity, self-knowledge and spirituality. In 1946, he received the Nobel Prize in Literature. Without a shadow of a doubt, you will have grown up with some of your favourite children's tales such as *Cinderella, Sleeping Beauty, Rapunzel, Little Red Riding Hood, Hansel and Gretle,* and of course *Snow White.* We all know that these children's tales come from folklore in some distant past, told from elder to elder, one household to another, generation to generation. But what you might not know, the fact that all of these stories would have not existed in their current form, had it not been for two brothers Jakob and Wilhelm Grimm (1785–1863) and (1786–1859), who are considered to be among the first to collect and publish a series of *Children's Household Tales* in 1812 and in 1815.

German philosophers

When I think of Germany as a country, one of the first things that comes to mind is its long-standing tradition of being a nation of thinkers. Unsurprisingly, the country has produced a long list of philosophers over the past few centuries, whose works have had a major influence on modern European philosophy: Kant, Hegel, Marx, Wittgenstein, Nietzsche, Heidegger, to name a few. Indeed, these old chaps formed the majority of the pillars which form our *raison d'etre* today.

Linguistically, it makes perfect sense, too: German language is the most logically structured, the most unambiguous, the most literal and the least visceral of all languages. Words mean exactly what they are supposed to mean, and compound nouns can go on forever, as I already explained in Chapter 4. Thus, as long as you follow the grammar rules, you can discover the meaning of any word and any sentence, without having to worry about figurative language and hidden meanings.

During my time at the University of Durham (a well-respected establishment, known for being one of the elite universities in the UK, alongside Cambridge, Oxford, Edinburgh and few others), where snobby public school students pride themselves on being at the top of the academic food chain, I remember having to read books by German scholars such as Theodor W. Adorno (1903-1969) for our music history module. It's the kind of book where one sentence takes up the whole page, and it took me about an hour to get through it (that one page). After struggling for months, I discovered that there was another book by an English scholar, which was specifically written to *simplify* the book by Adorno; *the Adorno for Dummies,* if you like. This book made a little more sense than the original, but it was still very painful to get through. At the time, I could not fathom why somebody would use such incredibly complex language. But that was before I moved to the federal republic. Moral of this short story — Germans do not like wasting time on simplifying things. To them, the world is a complex place that provokes complex ideas and thoughts. Simplifying them would be akin to degenerating to a lower level; devolutionising — if there is such a word — the dumbing down of human thought. Complex ideas need the supporting complexity of language, the German mantra goes. This is probably one of the reasons Facebook, Twitter, or TikTok could never have been created by a German.

Important Germans:

Kant & Nietzsche

Perhaps the most well-known and also the biggest polar opposites of German philosophers are Immanuel Kant (1724-1804) and Friedrich Nietzsche (1844-1900). Kant was best known for his pacifism and his belief in the *good* nature of human beings. Nietsche was the opposite; he appealed to our dark and nihilistic side, even supporting the idea of the Ubermensch, and by that I don't mean people who drive Ubers. A bit like Yoda and Darth Vader from the Star Wars trilogy. I am grossly simplifying of course, and I can already feel the wrath of academics on the back of my neck for making such a complex topic into such a rudimentary explanation. But I think the basic idea is there for everyone to understand.

Sigmund Freud (1856-1939)

One other significant milestone, which developed in the 20th Century, and can be attributed to a German speaker, is in the field of Psychology. At the end of the 19th Century, a man from Austria named Sigmund Freud (1856 – 1939) laid the groundwork for what is now commonly known as *modern psychology*. At the time when crazy people were still treated with ice picks stuck through their eyelids, Freud instead devised a method known as psychoanalysis, which is still a widely-used technique of treating psychosomatic illness through dialogue between patient and a psychoanalyst. You might wonder at this stage, why am I mentioning an Austrian neurologist in a book about Germany. The reason is, to put it simply – the language. It is no secret that all German-speaking countries have been under one umbrella in many respects, and I sincerely believe that Freud's accomplishment can be bundled under that *confederation* as well.

Religion

Christianity is the dominant religion in Germany, with 65 to 70 percent of the population identifying themselves as Christian. As a general rule of thumb, the southern federal states are primarily Catholic, while the northern *Bundesländer* tend to follow the Protestant tradition. And in stark contrast to a number of European countries, most notably neighbouring France, Germany still feels like quite a *Christian country*. Indeed, the centuries of religious fervour that were imposed upon its god-fearing people can still be felt in many parts of everyday life in Germany, irrespective of whether you're religious yourself or not. There are plenty of examples of this: consider things like the fact that 'religious' people still pay church taxes; shops remain resolutely closed on Sundays; by far the majority of public holidays in Germany have religious roots; and — most visibly — there are a heck of a lot of churches in Germany compared to other European nations. But how did it all begin (if you'll excuse the allegory)?

Martin Luther (1483-1546)

Until the 16th Century, Germany was omnipresently a Catholic nation. Then, along came a little known monk by the name of Martin Luther, who began the Protestant Reformation, effectively becoming one of the most influential and controversial figures in the history of Christianity. His 95 Theses, nailed to a church door in 1517, became the cornerstones of the Protestant beliefs, sparking the ensuing Protestant reformation. Today, 50% of Christians in Germany consider themselves Catholics, while the other 50% are Evangelical-Protestant. Geographically, most of the Catholics are in the south and the west of Germany, while the Protestants are in the North and East Germany. Another common trend: people in the big cities like Berlin and Hamburg tend to be non-religious, while rural areas, particularly in the South and West have a religious majority.

Good to know:

Germany is one of the few countries in the world that imposes a church tax on its citizens. This happened because of the nationalisation of religious property. In other words, churches in Germany are state-owned and require public funding to maintain. The tax is somewhere between 8 and 9 percent of your salary, depending on which Bundesland you live in. In 2018, the government collected 600 million euros in church taxes, the highest amount on record. Thus, if you ever plan on filling out a tax return in the Bundesrepublik, you will notice a section asking you about your religion. Incidentally, only Catholics, Protestants and Jews are subject to this tax. All others, including Muslims, Buddhists, Maoists, or even Jedi, do not have to worry about the extra expense, at least for now. If you want to avoid paying this, you'll need to opt out of it by ticking the relevant box in your income tax statement.

German history: a really short version

If you take a stroll through Hamburg towards the harbour area — somewhere between *Landungsbrücken* and the red light district of St. Pauli, you'll notice a tall statue of an old man with a bushy moustache, wearing a cape and holding a sword. The man is looking out toward the harbour, his gaze firmly fixed on the horizon. The monument is of Otto von Bismarck (1815-1898), known as the first chancellor, or the guy who in 1871 was largely responsible for the unification of the German Empire — the country as we now know it. Up to that point, Germany consisted of autonomous German-speaking kingdoms, principalities, free cities, bishoprics, and duchies. The monument is made of granite and was completed in 1906 by a sculptor by the name of Hugo Lederer. Despite the fact that they were officially 'unified' over 150 years ago, many German states still harbour a feeling of fierce independence; partly due to their historical importance to Germany, and partly due to their economical contribution to the country. Hence why the Hamburgers always look down on the *shabby* Berliners, who in turn view the Hamburgers as snobby *fish-heads*. Similarly, the Ruhr area considers itself the heart of German industry — the *mother* of all factory production, which includes coal, machinery, steel, cars and trains, whilst Bavaria has always viewed itself as an autonomous province, and thus continues to exert considerable political influence over the German federal government while turning its nose up at the rest of the country's citizens.

The fifty years of vacation

In the popular satire animation *Family Guy,* there is an episode where the two protagonists — Brian and Stewie — are enjoying the sites on a tour bus in Munich. The Bavarian tour guide, dressed appropriately in *lederhosen* and a traditional hat, gets very offended when quizzed about the tour pamphlet, which is lacking any information about the years 1939 to 1945, retorting that "nothing bad happened", and that "everybody was on vacation". The scene eventually culminates with the tour guide flying into a rage and shouting quasi-Nazi slogans in German with his arm outstreched in a Hitler salute. Although this scene had me rolling in stitches for hours, and would probably have a similar effect on many expats, I shouldn't think the Germans find it the least bit funny.

As historians will confirm, in the first half of the twentieth century, Germany did not make itself very popular with the rest of the world. Looking at the country today, it is still hard to fathom how much it endured during the twentieth century: first poverty and famine; then the emergence of the Third Reich and twelve years of rule under a fascist dictatorship; total annihilation in not one, but two, world wars; and the subsequent hold of communism over the East, which lasted for decades. It is staggering that Germany not only managed to come back from this, but to actually establish itself as the economic powerhouse of Europe and, moreover, as a towering model of democracy — all in less than thirty years, give or take. How is that possible, you might ask? The oversimplified answer – it could only have happened in a country like Germany, with a German mentality. We'll return to this idea in Chapter 7.

The Unification of 1989

After its defeat in World War II, Germany was managed by the Allied forces — France, the United Kingdom, the United States of America, and of course the Soviet Union. In 1961, a wall was built along the eastern border, effectively dividing Germany into two countries — the *Federal Republic of Germany* (West), and the not-so-democratic *German Democratic Republic* (East). As most of you will probably know, the wall stayed standing for twenty-eight years. Overnight, people woke up to the harsh reality of being separated from their families, without a chance to say goodbye to them. For many years, Berlin served as a hotspot for Cold War mind game battles between the Soviets and the Americans. If you're interested in the Berlin Wall, *then a visit to the Checkpoint Charlie Museum* in the centre is a must. In fact, I would recommend visiting Berlin to anyone with even the remotest interest in the subject of history: it is a fascinating place — a mecca for historic monuments, museums and heritage sites, and you could easily spend several days going from place to place.

The German political system

If you ever decide to watch German politicians on the telly, don't count on being entertained. It's far from the hysterical scenes in the US, where the (former) president turned politics into some kind of daytime soap opera. Nor is it the House of Lords in the UK, which is like watching a scene from *Harry Potter,* with people booing each other or shouting "hear hear" in an orgasm of approval. And it is definitely nothing like Ukrainian Parliament, where full-blown fist fights break out practically every week, fuelled by personal insults beginning with words like "Your mama is…" Indeed, German politicians are courteous, polite, well-educated, mostly disciplined, measured, and, well, quite boring — like you'd expect politicians to be. Quite a contrast to 1930s.

Germany is a federal republic, governed by a constitutional democracy. This means that the framework of rules which determines where power lies, and how people are elected, is described by a core document — the *Grundgesetz*. Unlike other constitutions, the *Grundgesetz* is regularly amended to adapt to the ever changing domestic and global environment. Germany is governed by its chancellor, usually the head of the majority party in the *Bundestag* (the house of parliament). Despite that, the country does have a president — but this job is primarily a ceremonial one, since the president does not possess any real political power. Instead, they are seen as the guardian of the German constitution, and they have to give their approval to every new chancellor.

As well as a federal government, each federal state in Germany — that is, each *Bundesland* — has its own state government and state premier *(Ministerpresident)*. State governments share power with the federal government and are in charge of things like protecting local identities, power and culture, and making important decisions about education and taxation. There are sixteen federal states in Germany. The largest is North Rhine-Westphalia, with over seventeen million inhabitants, while the smallest — Bremen — has just 670,000. Below the federal states sit the municipalities, which make decisions at an even more local level.

Reflecting these three tiers of government in Germany, there are three different types of elections: federal elections, during which politicians are elected to the *Bundestag*, take place every five years; state elections, which elect representatives to the state government *(Landtag)*, take place every four or five years; and local elections, which elect regional and local leaders like mayors, take place every four or five years. There are also EU elections, which take place every five years to select Germany's representatives in the European parliament. If you are a European citizen, you are allowed in both the local and European elections, but not in the federal or state ones.

Fig. 3 Political parties in the Bundestag

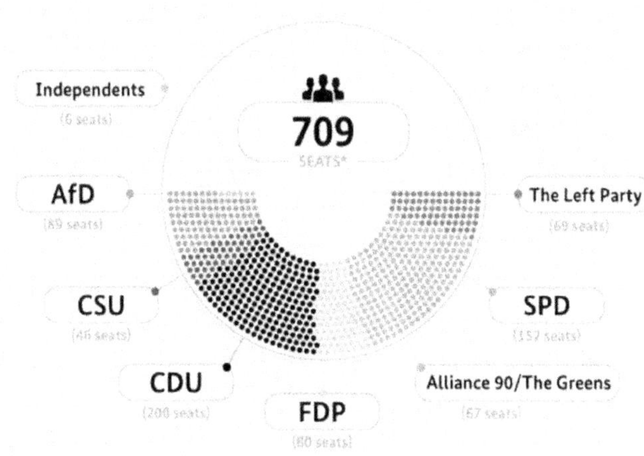

Source: https://www.tatsachen-ueber-deutschland.de/en/
politics-germany/parliament-parties

Currently, these are the major political parties in Germany:

- **Christian Democrats (CDU/CSU):** Located on the centre-right, the CDU and its Bavarian sister party, the CSU, have long been Germany's most electorally successful party. Founded in 1945 by a coalition of anti-Nazi groups and conservatives, the party brings together Protestants and Catholics, and generally follows pro-market, socially conservative policies. Famous figures include Angela Merkel (the current chancellor), Helmut Kohl and Konrad Adenauer.

- **Social Democrats (SPD):** The SPD is Germany's oldest party, and its second largest. Founded in 1863, the party was once Marxist-influenced but has become more moderate in the past fifty years. Nowadays, it lies in the centre ground and tends to propose social protections for workers, greater environmental regulation, and socially liberal policies.

- **Green Party:** Germany has one of the most successful Green parties in the world. Greens like Joschka Fischer have served as Foreign Minister, pushing Germany towards support for peace and pro-renewable policies. Thanks to their influence, Germany is on course to become a world-leading country for renewable energy, having committed to phase out both coal and nuclear power by the middle of the twenty-first century.

- **Free Democrats (FDP):** Positioned to the right of the CDU economically, but socially very liberal, the

FDP is hard to place in German politics. Founded in 1948 and currently headed by Christian Lindner, it regularly wins 7-8 percent in elections.

- **Die Linke:** Created in 2007 by left-wing dissidents in the SDP, Die Linke is a left-wing party that draws inspiration from anti-capitalist thinkers. Successful in the post-Communist East, it holds over sixty *Bundestag* seats.

- **Alternative for Germany (AfD):** Highly controversial, AfD is a right-wing nationalist party that seeks to reduce immigration and voices strong anti-Islam sentiments. It has few allies in other parties, which tend to work together to reduce its growth and influence. In recent years, however, the AfD has gained its highest number of seats in the *Bundestag* (96), amounting to 12.6 percent of the vote share. This has been largely attributed to Angela Merkel's decision to engage in an open-door policy during the refugee crisis; in 2015 alone, more than 890.000 asylum seekers came to Germany.

Chapter 6
Dating, Relationships & Family

Now we'll assume that by this point you've equipped yourself with some basic general knowledge about Germany, which exceeds the boundaries of doing a funny Hitler impression and saying things like *"Hände hoch"* (hands up). You have finally matured, and are feeling ready to properly integrate with *Ze Germanz* — and that may also involve meeting that special someone; a future partner or even a spouse. Well, my friend, you're ready for the dating game. But before you embark on that exciting journey, I thought I would share some personal stories, even some embarrassing ones, which will hopefully give you some helpful tips with regard to dating German men and women.

State your intentions

If you have read up to this point, it's probably already clear to you that words like spontaneity, ambiguity and surprise have no place in Germany — full stop. It's a sure way to get people annoyed with you, and this is also true when it comes to dating and sex. Imagine you're dating a girl; you meet for a drink for the first date, and then invite her back to your place for the second date. You've just opened up a takeaway menu, ready to choose your dish, when all of a sudden you hear the question:

"What are your romantic and sexual intentions?"

"Ehm **gulp** gee, I don't know. Could you ask me again after I've had food and downed this three-euro bottle of red from Penny?"

Take the same situation in a different country — let's use the UK as an example — the two amorous doves would rely much more on body language, chemistry, and subtle signals to act as indicators as to the other person's real *intentions*. Nobody would dream of being so direct, as most likely such actions would simply scare the other person away and ruin any chance of this relationship progressing further.

Although it may sound direct, it's not uncommon for people in Germany to ask questions like that, just to be absolutely clear. But don't think of it necessarily as a bad thing. In fact, there are distinct advantages, since following the rules, being predictable, unambiguous and very clear will ensure that you never find yourself in an awkward situation where you interpreted or read something that wasn't there. You'll never be in the position of thinking you're going to *get some,* only to find out that the other person was just being friendly. Everything is clear-cut and, in a way, this reflects the very blueprint of German society. Just like an equation: A leads to B, B leads to C, and so on.

I still remember, as if it were yesterday, the shock I got the first time I watched a German porno. I must have been in my late teens — so, yes, it was a very long time ago. The couple were making out; the woman was sitting on top of the man, who was sitting upright in an armchair. Suddenly, the dude said, *"Darf ich dich ficken?!"* (May I f*ck you?!) Forget the heat, the smooth transition from kissing to intercourse. Forget spontaneity, excitement, flirtation and so on. All of that went out of the window with one not so subtle sentence. What followed was less of a sexual scene, and more like watching a televised operation from a hospital theatre. Each new act was announced well ahead of time, with an exact description of what was coming.

Dude: *Ich werde nun deine Brüste mit meinen Händen in Uhrzeigerrichtung massieren* (I am now going to massage your breasts with my hands clockwise) — Because she was probably worried he'd be doing it with his feet — anti-clockwise.
Lady: *Oh ja* (Oh yes).
Dude: *Ich werde jetzt mein Penis in deine Muschi reinstecken* (I'm now going to insert my penis into your vagina).
Lady: *Oh ja.*
Dude: *Jetzt ist es drin* (Now it's in).
Lady: *Oh ja.*
And so it went on.

The reader may be forgiven for thinking that this scene was also shot for a "sexy podcast" (if such a thing exists) — and the director merely wanted to save time — shooting two birds with one stone, so to speak. But those more accustomed to German traits should know better. The commentary accompanying every action is definitely a German trait, like it or not.

Similarly to this robotic imitation of an erotically-charged encounter, the act of sex between seasoned couples in Germany (provided they are still doing it) often sounds more like a chore; an activity that you place in your calendar for a set day every week, which has to be observed by both parties in order to preserve a healthy relationship. The conversation might go like this:

Her: Darling, it's quarter to eight now, time for our weekly sexual activity.
Him: Yes, indeed, you are correct, I have already been thinking about naked women, and my penis is perfectly erect.
Her: Good, that will save us some time and we can get back to the couch in time for Tatort. Him: That's exactly my thinking.

Indeed, it's very common for couples in Germany to plan their sexual activity, even doing things like putting it in their joint calendar (I'm not joking). Another popular time for coitus is between the main course and the dessert, hence the name *inter-course* — excuse the pun.

Men sit down while they pee

A while back, I remember a friend of mine telling me a traumatic story about this girl he was dating from Hannover. He'd been seeing her for a few months, met her friends and apparently for a while everything was going in the right direction. That is, until one fine day when things started going rapidly *south*. He told me a vivid story about how they had had a romantic dinner, and then started smooching on the sofa, which naturally progressed into the sexual act (it wasn't the first time, he was very clear about that). They were at it for a few minutes when suddenly she stood up and disappeared into the bedroom. After a few minutes, she returned with a book. She opened it on a page that she had marked by neatly folding down the corner, a page which contained a graphical image of a vagina. It was the kind of a picture you would expect to see during a biology lesson, or that sex education class you had to take in your late teens. Without any hesitation, she then began pointing to various bits on the page, while tentatively explaining how the female orgasm works. She was calm and informative, similar to a friendly vacuum salesman, explaining the basics of how the *Dyson* really works. The poor guy was mortified; his ego shattered, and that pretty much spelled the end of that romantic evening, and the relationship itself.

Moral of the story: sex to Germans is a physical act akin to doing a workout, like running, rowing, climbing, or any other discipline you can think of. It has its own technique, rules and processes. Forget the mystery, the forbidden fruit, passion and anything else that is not actually tangible. That's all a pile of bollocks! As my friend told me his story, which had the unwritten title of 'Why he broke up with his girlfriend', I burst out laughing. It took me a good few minutes to come back to my senses. When I finally calmed down, I told him that I too had had a similar experience; I had once dated a girl who had viciously wounded my pride and my ego. Long story short, this girl and I got into a fierce argument because I didn't sit down to pee. Apparently, all German men are taught this from an early age, because it is hygienic, and bla, bla, bla. I refused, stating that 'just because women can't do it while standing, doesn't mean that men have to succumb to the toilet seat'. Let's just say, it didn't end well.

No macho-men here

You might remember reading earlier about the way German men behave at sports clubs. What has this got to do with a chapter on *dating, relationships and sex,* you might ask? I am just getting to that. In a stark contrast to the Brits, Australians, or the Americans, the Germans do not feel ashamed of *pampering* themselves in public. German men will use moisturiser in a public changing room, just because *it's good for their skin.* You'll also witness many men spending a considerable amount of time in front of the mirror, blow drying their hair. At times, I have had to awkwardly navigate through tight corridors, squeezing past other men while they are putting on their socks (before anything else), without a care in the world. Obviously, they've never heard of the 'soap in the shower' stories. In other words, the point I'm trying to make here is that German men, apart from being completely at ease with collective nakedness, do not fit the bill of what I've been taught is typically 'masculine'. Or at least, the concept of being all burly and manly is not part of their culture. The notion of a neanderthal alpha-male, whose role is to hunt for food, collect firewood and protect his territory from enemies, does not seem to be relevant in the modern game of finding a sexual mate, at least not here in the *Bundesrepublik.* The proverbial hunting axe has been swapped for the hair dryer, and the bow and arrow ditched in favour of body lotion. And I'm not saying that the changing rooms is a great example of how German men act around women. But it appears to me, at least in theory, that the traditional roles of men and women are not as prevalent as they are in Anglo-Saxon cultures. This is an interesting point and it may explain a lot of things in relation to the dating game in Germany.

Quite recently, there was a post in an expat group on Facebook, in which someone asked, quite openly, what expats thought about dating in Germany. What followed was nothing short of an avalanche of comments, ranging from widely-held assumptions about the lack of romance and the overly pragmatic approach, through to more absurd claims like "dating is dead on arrival" and that "German men have weird lumpy faces". Although this post was probably meant as a joke and the responses shouldn't be taken too seriously, one particular answer was posted several times by different people. Apparently, it's a popular opinion that German men are too shy when it comes to asking someone out. This opinion was reiterated by several people I interviewed for this book. If this is indeed the case, then it would go some way to explaining the assertiveness exercised by the opposite sex.

Kinky Germans

I feel really lucky to live in one of the nicest cities in Germany — Hamburg. Over the past century, a thriving maritime industry has made it into one of the richest cities in Germany. In stark contrast to the capital city Berlin, Hamburg boasts beautiful architectural marvels, shiny new buildings, old churches and a great transport system.

Hamburg is very clean, tidy and easy to navigate. Indeed, Hamburg is one of the most sought-after 'settling-down places' — very popular among Germany's rich and famous, including Dieter Bohlen (Modern Talking), Till Schweiger (the famous German actor) and Udo Juergens (a singing legend), not to mention many a private billionaire. Thus, it is not a coincidence that Hamburg is considered to have the most millionaires per capita in all of Europe. Almost seven million tourists — both foreign and domestic — visit the Hanseatic city (as it is officially known) every year, which helps to fill the coffers considerably.

In the heart of Hamburg is the *Reeperbahn,* the city's famous red light district; littered with clubs, bars, restaurants and theatres, and home to a great live music scene. Every famous German musician will have performed here. The Reeperbahn likes to boast that it's the place where 'the Beatles got famous', a quote which every bar and pub owner will repeat to you over and over again, so much so that entrepreneurial guides eventually started doing a *Beatles Tour,* which, I believe, is very popular.

The *Reeperbahn* may be best known for its brothels and strip clubs, but if you walked down it during the day, you'd be amazed to see a different side to the sex industry in full swing. Shop windows with neon blue, yellow and red lights, displaying words like 'porn' and 'sex', are not exactly hiding from public view. On the contrary, they flash loud and proud in almost all corners of the *Reeperbahn.* Contrary to the image I had when I lived in the UK — of the patrons of sex shops being middle-aged men dressed in long coats and sunglasses, with their hats pulled low over their eyes and hands in their pockets, hesitantly standing outside the premises on a meticulously planned incognito trip, on a carefully selected day, when their wifes and kids are away, having gone out of the back door, and taken a long detour, to make sure the neighbours were not watching, before finally summoning the courage and making a dash inside — the Germans are very open about their sexual cravings, as they are about sex in general (remember the *German Sauna* in Chapter 4?)

Standing outside of a sex shop on the *Reeperbahn*, you will notice couples of all ages, holding hands, stopping in front of windows in a spontaneous manner, as if something has just grabbed their attention, as if they are just pausing outside H&M to admire the selection of cocktail dresses — as if, in other words, peering into the window of a sex shop is nothing to be embarrassed about, far from it. Perhaps *Chanel* has just released their latest dildo collection, 'for him and for her', or *Versace* has just brought out their latest bondage set 'whip-du-jour'. In any case, the lack of embarrassment or coyness is quite astounding — or at least, it is to a tightly-laced Brit like me — and that goes for both partners. This also applies to the shop itself. The feel inside is more akin to a record shop, with its open, well-lit space, spacious aisles on both sides and clear signage for different niches:

Ground Floor: *Sex toys, Dildos, Strap-ons.*
Lower Ground Floor: *BDSM, Leather, Dominatrix*

I only stepped into a sex shop once in my life, and I had to google half of the categories displayed on the sign. Aside from the sex shops, there are other establishements like the 'Sex-Kino', strip clubs and 'drag shows', which are, incidentally, always sold out.

Between the Burger King and the police station on the *Reeperbahn*, you will often find a row of sex workers. They are easy to recognise thanks to their warm puffer jackets, bum bags, and long training pants. Not exactly what I would call the 'dress-to-impress' look. Then again, I don't think that's the look they are going for. In my twenties, when I went out partying on the *Reeperbahn* almost every weekend, my other male friends were often approached by sex workers. Their tactic was to come at them quickly from the side, put their arm into the man's elbow and say something along the lines of, "*Und was mit dir?*" (And what about you?) It used to happen to certain male friends almost every single time we went out, but never to me. I was quite offended at the time, thinking it was down to my looks, or perhaps I looked like a poor musician (which is exactly what I was), and they thought they would be wasting their time (which they would have been). Only later in my thirties did it dawn on me why I was never 'picked on', which, in retrospect, gave me a great sense of satisfaction and an ego boost. The answer is basically a combination of all of the above, and from that we can deduce that a perfect target would be a forty-plus male, with cash to burn, and not the kind you'd see on a Tommy Hilfiger summer collection catalogue.

There is a misconception in the world about Germans being the kings of bondage and other kinky stuff. I for one, also believed this to be true, so I had to google it. I typed 'kinkiest countries in the world' into Google search (a thing I will probably regret for the rest of my days, fully aware that some data-mining company will now be inundating me with BDSM adverts, or worse, that this information will somehow be used by Mark Zuckerberg and his chums against me in the future). I was quite surprised by what I found. According to www.thrillist.com, Germans are not even in the top ten for BDSM. It is actually the US, where 70 percent of the population is apparently into bondage. Not sure how they worked that out, but I'll bite (pun intended). I was even more surprised to find that the UK was top-ranked for 'spanking'. The Germans, however, do occupy a top spot for one of the categories — dirty talk, which I found to be quite ironic. Considering how they speak to each other in porn movies, I should imagine that listening to German *dirty talk* is about as erotic as cutting your toenails, but then again, I am not German.

Dating tips

Just like in any other language, there are certain rules for dating in German and it is important to observe these before embarking upon your adventure. Below are a few things to bear in mind:

- If you ask somebody out for a coffee, that means friends, and if you ask somebody out for a drink, that means a date, unless you order a beer.
- When asking someone out on a date, be specific. Name a date, a time and a place, as otherwise you might irritate the other party ahead of time. At least twenty-four hours before the date make sure you send a detailed description of the place where you're meeting, and an annotated map link and a pdf of the menu (if available). This shows to the other person that you are well organised, that you've thought of everything in advance, and obviously have serious and honourable intentions.
- When you're on the date, make sure that you listen attentively to everything the other person says. Repeat and paraphrase their stories, but make sure you don't interrupt them at any point. Always wait until they have finished their sentence. Try to mimic their facial expressions with your own.
- If you don't know what to talk about, use safe topics like insurance, or doctor's appointments, or look for further inspiration in my icebreakers chapter.
- When the cheque comes, always assume a split-bill;

do not insist on paying. If that happens, the German person might think that they owe you something and this will tip the balance in the wrong direction. You can politely ask if you may offer to buy the other person a drink: *"Darf ich dich einladen"* (Can I buy you a drink?), but be as eloquent as possible in the matter.

- When saying goodbye, make sure to plan another rendezvous, or alternatively state that you are going to be very busy for the next five months. Do not leave an open-end date. This will cause a turmoil in the other person. They will try to analyse everything that happened that evening in order to come to a conclusion about whether or not you will ask them out again. The one thing they won't do, however, is ask you themselves.

- When writing WhatsApp messages, be elaborate. Do not write short messages like "Hey" with a smiley face and expect a reply. Your messages must be at least three hundred characters, beginning with your full name, how you know the other person and what your intentions are. Below is an example with the important indicator words highlighted in bold.

> "Hello, this is **Fadi Gaziri** contacting you. We met at the **Schnitzeljagd** festival on the **3rd of June 2020.** It was quite sunny, but occasionally overcast. I had so much fun that day because when I tried to find the schnitzel, I tripped with my right foot over my left, and fell with my face

in the mud, it was very funny — ha, ha, ha. I thought that maybe you would like to meet for a **drink.** There is a cafe in **Jungfernstieg** called **Alex.** I can reserve a table there on **Friday 26th of July** (in 3 weeks from now) at **7:32 pm.** Alternatively, I can also do the following **Saturday,** the **first Friday in September,** or the **3rd Saturday in October,** whichever suits you best. I have included a map link below, as well as a link to a menu on their website, and a Google review link. I look forward to hearing from you. smiley face, wink, wink, Fadi Gaziri (PS. Fadi is my first name, Gaziri is my family name)."

- If you get lucky, there is no need to beat around the bush, use euphemisms, or code words such as "Do you wanna come in for a coffee". In fact, do not use the latter at all, as that will probably confuse your envisaged sexual partner. They might reply confusedly: "But I don't drink coffee at such a late hour", or something in that vein. Remember, in Germany everything is part of a logical equation (A+B=C). So, if you managed to get your variables right, then it's like a computer game. Once you've completed a level, you've unlocked the next one.
- Once you get down to the sexual act, you can scroll up to the bit about the 'German porno'. Start practicing.

Interviews

Due to the fact that my own experience in the area of relationships and dating in Germany can hardly be considered insightful, I thought it would be a good idea to get some real examples from some real-life couples. After all, what could be better than using actual people and their everyday situations? I decided to ask around, and since I am part of an expat community, it didn't take long to find some suitable candidates to extend an invitation to. To my delight, most of them accepted. I have to mention one minute detail: in order to qualify, one partner had to be German, and the other a foreigner. Here's what they had to say.

Maya and Torsten

Maya is Russian who has lived in Germany for over ten years. She teaches English and German at a state school. Her husband Torsten is German and works as an accountant for the UN. They live in the western part of Hamburg with their two boys, aged four and nine.

Q: *Could you tell us a bit about how you met your partner?*

M: We met at East Hotel during an InterNations event in June 2008. We were friends for a couple of years before we got together. Once things got serious, things went very quickly. We got married within six months (2011), when I was already pregnant with our first child, and bought our first house together the same year.

Q: *Is that typical for Germans?*

M: In my experience, German men are reserved. They bide their time, and need alcohol to get the ball rolling. But once they get serious, things start moving really fast.

Q: *Were there any culture clashes at first?*

M: In Russia, it is customary for men to give flowers to their girlfriends on 8th March. Torsten wasn't accustomed to that, and I had to teach him.

Q: *What makes your partner German in a relationship?*

M: Torsten arranges his spices alphabetically and gets annoyed if I misplace them. He also doesn't like it if I don't put his CDs back on the shelf. Also with regard to his parents: if you want to plan anything with them, you have to do it months in advance. They are retired, but they are always busy doing something.

Q: *Is there a clear division of roles in your relationship?*

M: No, we have a modern relationship, and do most things together. We don't have any set *roles* per se.

Q: *What advice (if any) would you give to other expats about being in a relationship with a German?*

M: Get some beers in, to get things moving.

Q: *Do Germans have any customs that you didn't know about?*

M: If a woman lights up a candle that means she has serious intentions.

Q: *Does your partner sit down to pee?*

M: Yes he does. He was well brought up.

Patrick and Antje

Patrick is a 39-year-old facility manager from Dublin, and Antje is a primary school teacher from the northern part of Germany, a place called Itzehoe. They live in central Hamburg with their two kids — a boy and a girl, five and ten years old, respectively.

Q: *Could you tell us a bit about how you met your partner?*

P: We met while backpacking in Australia, a country where every second tourist I met turned out to be German.

Q: *Were there any culture clashes at first?*

P: Yes, little things like what to eat and when. For me there isn't really a predefined time to eat. I'll eat when I'm hungry and any combination is fine as long as it tastes good to me.

Q: *So you get told off if you put things on a plate that don't really go together?*

P: Yeah, something like that. I'd be told "das passt nicht zusammen" (that doesn't fit together).

Q: *What makes your partner German in a relationship?*

P: Antje needs to have a plan — always. I already noticed it when we went backpacking together. Every detail had to be meticulously and thoroughly planned. After that holi day, I think I needed another one. Just kidding. No, I mean, there are lots of advantages with that too, which I mustn't forget. Another one is thriftiness, being really careful with money. In retrospect, in recent years, the roles have reversed, and I've become the "sparsam"(thrifty) one. I think it's Stockholm syndrome, perhaps? Oh, and not sure if it's a German thing, but the apartment has to be immaculate before the arrival of guests, heaven forbid if there's a tiny drop of urine on the toilet seat.

Q: *Seems like you've got quite a few points there already...*

P: Oh yeah, and one more, Germans hate to tip!

Q: *Do Germans have any customs that you didn't know about?*

P: Ahm, well something I didn't know before: it's not acceptable to buy a pre-cooked bird for your Christmas dinner for your guests. You have to really show that you had put in the effort.

Q: *Do you sit down to pee?*

P: Yes, been forced to over the years. Now it's become a habit. If there's one thing that's more important to Germans than the Schnitzeljagd and table manners, it's sitting whilst peeing!

Q: *What advice (if any) would you give to other expats about being in a relationship with a German?*

P: It's a tricky one. I suppose my advice for any man getting into a relationship with a German woman would be: be prepared to compromise on your machoness if you want this to work.

Donald and Judith

Donald is a 45-year-old American translator, who has lived in Germany for over twenty years. His wife Judith (31) grew up in Hamburg and works as a social worker. They currently live in an apartment with their two children, aged two and a half, and six months.

Q: *Could you tell us a bit about how you met your partner?*

D: We met on Tinder. We then met up in a hip part of town for a first date. One thing led to another very quickly. We were a couple in no time.

Q: *Were there any culture clashes at first?*

D: Nothing at first, no. Now we have some. Actually, a bit more than some. But maybe it has less to do with culture than with systems of belief and what we place importance on? What I can say is that my relationship to TV, movies and multimedia — something which is common and highly celebrated in the USA — is something that really irks her, and she doesn't accept it as a cultural difference she should just have to live with.

Q: *So, you basically mean that you grew up in front of the television?*

D: Yes, the TV was on pretty much all the time. As a kid, I would spend Saturday in front of the TV watching cartoons, like literally five to eight hours per day. My wife's upbringing involved very little television, so understandably, she goes nuts if the TV is even on for a half hour.

Q: *What makes your partner German in a relationship?*

D: She's very into punctuality, organisation, and proper manners. She's very against anything, even in pop culture, that could be associated with being antisocial or lazy. She also has a fairly German sense of humour and isn't open to much of what makes people laugh in other cultures. She grew up in one of the better neighborhoods around town and has some pretty fixed ideas on how a person should conduct themself in just about any situation in public and when there's company. I don't know if I'd classify that as German, per se, but it does lead to times when I think she's a bit snobby. And that's something I've encountered in many Germans.

Q: *What advice (if any) would you give to other expats about to get into a relationship with a German partner?*

D: Oh, this is a loaded question! I'll start by pointing out that there is an incredible amount of very attractive and intelligent women in the city I'm living in, much less in the rest of the country. Of the countries I've visited, Germany definitely ranks very high on my list of overall level of physical attractiveness. Now, I've been in Germany for many, many years and spent much of that time enjoying a single, party lifestyle. My experience is that there is a certain noticeable reservation and coldness in German women that I haven't always experienced with women of other nationalities. I've unfortunately also encountered a number of women who have had poor relationships with their fathers and the effects of that became very evident within a very short period of time. Furthermore, I've also unfortunately experienced a fairly heavy level of unhealthy possessiveness and this wasn't just a one-time occurrence. Now, these things may very well just be my experience or something that can be experienced with women everywhere, but alas, these experiences took place for me in Germany.

Q: *Do you sit down when you pee?*

D: Yes. I certainly do. And I always do it when visiting someone else's house/apartment. That generally all started when I had female flatmates, but I noticed that it's highly appreciated in many circles and that peeing standing up in someone else's place of residence is basically interpreted as an act of great disrespect.

Getting Married in Germany

Having touched upon the topic of dating and relationships, it's time to follow through the cycle chronologically, leading oh-so-naturally to the subject of marriage and children. Here, I'll examine the ins and outs of the prospect of getting hitched in Germany, and later follow that up with some observations about growing up in this country and the things that await your (future) children in the German school system.

Germany is an incredibly family-friendly and family orientated country. Whether you're talking about things like maternity or paternity leave, state subsidies for families, tenancy laws in favour of children, schools, tax breaks for families, or even urban planning - everything is done to make family living in this country as easy as possible, a welcoming thought for expats, I'm sure.

As an 'avid expat', I am also a member of no fewer than twelve expat groups on Facebook, and actively follow all of the different threads, trying to help where I can — or where I can be bothered. People post questions about all sorts of topics related to living in Germany. More often than not, the main reason they do that is because they are new or relatively new to the country, overwhelmed by the German language, rules and regulations, and — most importantly — getting very frustrated at not being able to get a *simple* answer to what they are looking for, in English. Oftentimes searching for an answer to a question in Germany only turns up more questions — it can get quite depressing indeed. If you managed to read through the *unemployment benefits* chapter in this book, then you'll know exactly what I mean.

The hard fact I have learned during my time in this country is that nothing is simple. It's as simple as that (if you'll excuse the pun). To put it in context, Germans do not like to simplify things; it's not in their nature. We've seen many examples of this throughout this book: whether it's the compound nouns resulting in excessively long words; the overcomplicated chains of command in German companies; the overly bureaucratic public system; or even things like the need to justify and comment on everything that is being said. Alas, this complexity applies to every aspect of life in Germany, and, although it does get easier with time, initially it can be quite astounding. Even once you do get used to it, every now and then a simple everyday situation which becomes needlessly complicated will force you to take a step back and say, "Hey, it doesn't have to be this way!" This is what happened when I got engaged in 2018. At first, my fiance and I looked at the possibility of getting hitched in Germany. I called countless municipal offices, citizen's advice bureaus, and spent hours reading through the official guidelines. It quickly became very clear to us that it was a mammoth task that involved a lot of paperwork. All of our supporting documents had to be legally translated into German, stamped at a municipality office, and in some cases even ratified by a regional court. And even after you manage to get all of that done, the waiting lists for civil ceremonies can take up to a year and a half in major cities like Hamburg, Munich, Berlin or Cologne. Church services even longer. It's enough to deter you from getting married full stop.

Luckily, only a few hours further north, Germany borders Denmark, a small Scandinavian country with a population that barely reaches five million, and, unsurprisingly, a very popular destination for foreigners to get married. After loading up Copenhagen's official council website, I sent an email inquiring about a possible date. This was mid-October. Within a few weeks, we had a date confirmed at the beginning of February the following year; i.e., in three months' time. I was shocked at how simple and uncomplicated this seemed — almost too good to be true. So I called them up. The conversation went a bit like this:

Me: Hello, my name is Fadi Gaziri and I'm calling about a case number 12345 regarding the marriage of XY, and the email reply that we received on 12th November 2019.

Thune: Yes, we received your application, and allocated your first choice date of 2nd February 2020.

Me (a bit shell-shocked): So you don't require any more paperwork, translations, or any other supporting documents?!

Thune: Nope, you're all set, we'll send you a reminder email a month before with documents you have to bring in original to the wedding ceremony.

Me: Buuut....I....if....how?

Thune: It's okay, a lot of people from Germany have that reaction, we're used to it. Have a nice day, and give us a call if you have any other questions.

Me: Ahmmmm, ok, thhhhank you, have a nnnnice day you too.

Should you decide to go through the ordeal in Germany, for whatever reasons, make sure you start planning at least eighteen months ahead of your wedding. Perhaps, now that you know how much planning is involved, it might seem more logical to you that somebody would ask "what are your intentions" as early as a second date — if you're going to get the paperwork sorted in time, you'd better get a move on! I've included a list of documents required to get married in Germany (both parties):

- *A valid passport*
- *An official birth certificate*
- *Proof of a minimum of 21 days' continuous residence in Germany (this can be a Meldebescheinigung issued by the local Anmeldeamt)*
- *Proof of being single (Ledigkeitsbescheinigung)*
- *Birth certificates of children (if any) the couple have together*
- *The required application and questionnaire from the Standesamt*
- *Certificate of No Impediment (CNI) (Befreiung vom Ehefähigkeitszeugnis)*
- *Marriage certificates from previous marriages*
- *A financial statement*

On top of the time it takes to get all these documents sorted, you need to factor in a waiting time of anything between six months and a year and a half, depending on where in Germany you live.

Having children: The German way

Until as recently as 2019, the birthrate in Germany was consistently low, hovering at about 1.54 children per woman. Thus, it is not surprising that the German government has been actively encouraging procreation by putting various financial incentives in place. These include things like a generous parental allowance package for both mother and father; various tax breaks for families; and even paid vacations. With this in mind, it is hardly surprising that Germans become such expert family planners. Before they even 'get down to business' with their partner with the aim of making a baby, they will have learnt how to work the system to their benefit, and worked out the most efficient, cost-effective and timely way to have children. In other words, the decision is entirely not spontaneous, but one that takes rigorous planning, sometimes years in advance. You might think that's a bit exaggerated, but I am actually speaking from experience. At one point in my life I was dating a student lawyer who, after we had been going out for less than a year, began mapping out our shared future for the next five to ten years, which I thought was a bit hasty, to say the least. The discussion about kids involved a complicated matrix of factors; with various different scenarios based upon which grade she ended up with after her second and final year exams, and whether she would get a job at a top law firm, or her second or even third choice. Other essential steps that needed to be planned down to the last detail were spending a certain number of years in permanent employment before the first child, buying a house, getting a dog, and having a second child — all in that order. I felt like my life was being planned for me and I was just a back-seat passenger. Shockingly, that relationship didn't last.

My wife and I currently occupy a 2.5 bedroom apartment on the second floor of an old-style building known as *Altbau.* These buildings are very popular amongst Germans, mainly because they were built at the beginning of the century with high ceilings, lavish fixtures, spacious rooms, original wooden floors, large windows, and are the complete opposite to the ugly *Platte* (buildings built as a matter of urgency after World War II, for the sole purpose of providing living space for Germany's population). The apartment is perfect for two people — we have a bedroom, a small kitchen, a bathroom, a living room, and a study where I do most of my daily work. Although there are great advantages to living in an *Altbau* building, there are also distinct drawbacks — namely, it can be very noisy. The insulation of the floors is poor, and the wooden boards reverberate like bombshells when something falls on them. As Murphy's law would have it, the same space above us is occupied by a five-person household (two adults, three kids), which is highly unorthodox for the Germans – in the *geist* of *planning ahead,* so to speak. Most of the time there is no issue, but now and again my supply of reason and *c'est la vie* runs dry, and a mixture of anger, rage and self-pity take their place (usually about the time when I tell 'Alexa' to play heavy metal on full blast). Surprisingly enough, this works like a charm. Anyway, slightly off-topic now. The original point I was making was that this family had obviously not read the *German Handbook* on having children, and decided to bring up three kids in an apartment that is barely big enough for a couple. Taking into account the fact that the guy works in a music store, and supports his whole family on that income, and maybe, a few gigs a month, it's pretty safe to say that they are unlikely to move anytime soon, and thus, we have two options: either we move ourselves, or we'd have to put up with the noise for years to come (until their kids grow up). Either way, I did the German thing, and read up on the 'neighbour regulations' – I'm not saying I would call the *Ordnungsamt*, but at least it's comforting to know that I could. Oh, I forgot to mention – the father of the family above us is English.

Did you know:

Germany is the only country in the world that offers a parent-child vacation paid for by the state. This allowance is available to any parent whose child does not exceed the age of twelve, and can be applied for once every four years.

In many ways, the school system in Ger-

Adolescence, upbringing & the German school system

many encapsulates its society; it shows how 'the powers that be' think it should be structured; how they want people's minds to work; and the kind of values they want to instill into their population.

After almost a year working as a supply teacher in

a school, my contract came to an end. After deliberating for a while, I decided to get a full teacher's qualification. The main reason was not financial, but rather that I felt as though I finally needed to grow up and get myself some job security. Having been a freelance musician for most of my adult life, I have never really had a problem living with financial uncertainty. This was mainly due to the fact that I was fairly successful in my field of work, having built a steady network over the years. I had plenty of work, I travelled a lot and enjoyed lots of freedom. But as you get older — and yes, I'm going to do the *as-you-get-older spiel* — I got tired of travelling on my own. I got sick of hotels and their sterile and neutral decor and their pompous rich guests, of having to perform songs to strangers I would never meet again. I got sick of cruise ships and safety drills, having to stand there in uniform every week, pretending to care about the guests, but secretly wishing the ship would sink, along with all of their whining and complaining. I got sick of dealing with power-grabbers and sociopaths, the kind of people who try to make your life miserable if you rub them up the wrong way. I got sick of airports and airport lounges, with their astronomically priced coffee and their uncomfortable chairs. I developed an insidious hatred for passengers who get up as soon as the boarding announcement is made, fearful that there will not be enough seats for everyone or enough space for their precious carry-on bags. I also developed a certain indifference to new places. I became allergic to crowds of people and yearned for my own quiet retreat where I could escape it all. To summarise — it was time for yet another major change.

During the summer of 2019, I applied for a teaching course, which in Germany is similar to a conversion course in the UK. It is aimed at professionals with Master's degrees, and allows them to attain a teacher's qualification within a shortened period of eighteen months. The course combines part-time teaching at a designated school along with seminars and additional training. The assessments are carried out in the form of a so-called Hospitation — basically, your seminar leader and your mentors assessing you in the classroom during an actual lesson. Everything is fairly straightforward.

One thing I noticed is that, in Germany, when you tell people you're a teacher, there always follows a kind of aura of silence: not the awkward kind of silence that you'd get if you told people you work in the porn industry (not that I've ever witnessed anyone confessing to that), but one that is half filled with respect, and half filled with pity. Both emotions are provoked by the assumption that you're incredibly courageous — or perhaps incredibly stupid — for having chosen a profession where your days will be filled with the sound of screaming children; your afternoons with PTAs chock full of over-protective parents, who will vehemently deny that their little darling could kick the shit out of his classmates with words like, "My little Kevin would never do such a terrible thing"; and your evenings with correcting homework. You may get an extraordinary number of days off per year, but you'll spend most of them sitting in your tiny, cubicle-esque garden with your thirty-year mortgage tied around your neck like a tombstone, watching enviously how your two labradors are having a way better life than you, and reminiscing back to the days when you could get up at eleven am with absolutely nothing planned for the day. But let's put that aside for the moment and take a look at the German school system.

From the tender age of seven, all German children go to elementary school, which is known as *Grundschule*. After that, they are inaugurated into the secondary school system, which covers grades 5 to 13 and educates children between the ages of eleven and nineteen. The main types of secondary school establishments are the *Hauptschule*, the *Realschule*, the *Gymnasium*, and the *Gesamtschule* (sometimes also called a *Stadtteilschule*). While the *Hauptschule* and the *Realschule* focus more on vocational qualifications, the higher-ranked *Gymnasium* is for 'academic' students and usually leads to an *Abitur*, which is a prerequisite for attending an academic university in Germany. The *Gesamtschule* is a kind of comprehensive school that combines all of these education types and is gradually becoming more prevalent. Contrary to in some countries where papers are graded from A to F, in Germany the grading system is a numerical one. The higher the number, the lower the grade. So, for example, the very top mark is a 1.0. To study law or medicine at university, a student would require a top grade somewhere between around 1.0 and 1.5. The city of Hamburg has a total of about 900 secondary schools (*Gymnasien* and *Stadtteilschule*). Typically every school has between 900 and 1000 pupils, which is about 115 pupils per year with four classes of twenty-seven pupils. A normal figure by anyone's standards.

In Germany, the dates for school holidays differ slightly de-

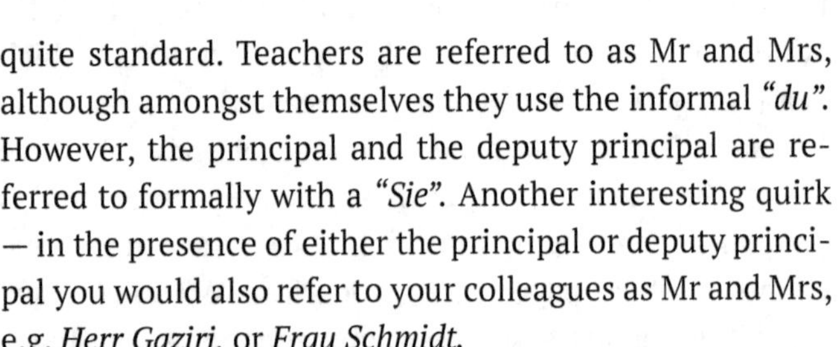

Good to know:

pending on which state you're in. It is a simple, but absolutely genius system, which is primarily designed to prevent the whole country from going on a holiday at the same time. This makes perfect sense in so many ways that I can't believe more countries haven't followed suit.

The code of conduct at school is also

quite standard. Teachers are referred to as Mr and Mrs, although amongst themselves they use the informal *"du"*. However, the principal and the deputy principal are referred to formally with a *"Sie"*. Another interesting quirk — in the presence of either the principal or deputy principal you would also refer to your colleagues as Mr and Mrs, e.g. *Herr Gaziri,* or *Frau Schmidt.*

During my very first stint as a teacher — when I was still working as a temp supply teacher at a *Stadtteilschule* — I was asked at one point to attend a disciplinary hearing for one of my pupils. The subject in question was an 11-year-old girl who had broken the school rules on several occasions and had been disrupting classes. She was a cute little girl with long blonde hair, who liked to sing Ariana Grande, and was obviously one of the more popular girls in her class. When I got to the principal's office, she was already sitting there with her mother. It was apparent that the family consisted of a working-class single mother who was never home, working temp jobs and barely managing to pay bills (she told us this later). Thus the girl was left on her own most of the time. Once everyone — including the 11-year-old girl, her mother, seven adult teachers, and one principal — was seated at a round table, the session began akin to a court hearing. The principal stated the facts in a very cordial way, using formal language. After that, every teacher went on to berate the poor girl individually, telling her what she had done wrong, and telling her why they were *upset* with her. I had never witnessed anything like it in my entire life. Within minutes, the girl was in tears, while her mother was trying to justify her behaviour, talking about her life situation, the lack of work, and the impact of being a single parent. This went on for about half an hour, after which the principal suggested some measures for improvement. These included the girl changing class. She was also given a formal written warning, which is a standard procedure, which could eventually lead to her being expelled from the school, if another such incident occurred.

To be quite truthful, I was in shock. I felt so sorry

for the girl, overwhelmed by not one, not two, but seven of her teachers, all telling her off. I thought to myself that if I had been a parent in that situation, I would have probably kicked the shit out of half of the people in that room, pardon my outburst. I also thought about the fact that the girl would probably be scarred for life after such an ordeal; the emotional and psychological trauma that such an event would cause in the life of an eleven-year-old would be devastating. In the weeks to come, I saw the same girl outside in the school yard, but it seemed as though she had been substituted by a twin sister. She seemed subdued, with her head down as she walked around the school. She wasn't playing with other girls, and her cheeky little smile had completely vanished from her face. I also found out that she had been transferred to another class, and was no longer in my music class. I felt quite sad indeed.

There are many behaviour traits exhibited by German adults that I have always found a bit 'annoying', to say the least. One of those is the fact that you're always expected to listen to whatever drivel they are saying, right through to the end, and not interject or interrupt at any point. This relates to almost any setting — be it a conversation between two people about the weather; a chat to your supervisor at work; a phone conversation with somebody trying to sell you something; a political debate on television; or even a full-blown argument on the street. There is never a point where you'll hear anyone interrupting the other, which is a bit odd, especially in the latter two examples. But since I began working as a teacher in the German school system, I finally learnt where this strange habit originates — at school.

The etiquette of allowing pupils to speak without shutting them up exists there too. It never ceases to amaze me just how much time and effort teachers dedicate to preserving this mantra. I have never heard a teacher shout, use moderately foul language like "shut it", or even snap at a pupil, be it a fifth grader, or one of the seniors. Teachers — in my school at least — are always patient with pupils, and tend to explain pretty much everything, even to the young ones. There is never a time when a teacher drops his or her guard and replies dismissively to some stupid remark a pupil has made. And if it ever comes to punishment, teachers always make sure that the pupil understands exactly why he or she has been sent out of class, or told to stay behind and mop up the floor.

On the one hand, this approach teaches young adults respect and solidarity toward their peers and adults alike, which is certainly encouraging. On the other hand, it explains why people in Germany always expect everything to be explained to them, down to the smallest detail. No questions ever remain unanswered, no stones unturned. Nothing remains 'up in the air', and there is no room for ambiguity, ambivalence or — quite frankly — your own interpretation. Try to explain the meaning of *read between the lines* to a German and it will feel like hitting your head against a very large rock — and the result will be similar. But this lack of ambiguity does not necessarily mean that they are succinct. Quite to the contrary. As I mentioned above, people will happily talk and talk for hours without anyone ever asking them to 'put a sock in it'. If you try to apply the English model of 'talking over a person', otherwise known as *filibustering*, you'll be amazed to find that your opposite will continue talking, long after you've finished, at exactly the same pace, tone and volume. So that strategy won't work.

Another important notion which forms a cornerstone of German upbringing is to get pupils as young as eleven to reflect on all their deeds and actions. Here in Germany they call it *reflektieren*, i.e. thinking about what you've done, and the effect it has had on you and the people around you. This process is built-in to almost every lesson, and is part of the *teacher's manual*. Essentially it works akin to writing up a methodology in a science experiment — documenting every part of it— and then suggesting improvements that you could implement next time; a conclusion of the sorts. At school, pupils are asked to do this as part of their lesson, usually at the end, and often in written form. The teacher then uses this *self-reflection* as part of the overall assessment: did the pupil understand what went wrong, and did they acknowledge this in their report? Did he or she take the right steps to achieve the result? Did he or she understand how the result came about? So much importance is given to this part of the learning process that in many cases pupils end up thinking that it is more important to write up a good 'reflection' than actually do a good experiment and get a result. With that in mind, I wouldn't be surprised if that poor 11-year old girl I mentioned earlier is going to be *reflecting* for the rest of her life, most likely in a one-to-one session with a cognitive behaviour therapist.

Do you see where I'm heading with this *smirk*? Let me remind you of my rant earlier in the book about the Germans being more concerned with the *process* over the *result*. Perhaps now you're on the same page as me. I know it is too far-fetched to assume that all Germans put the process above the results because they think having a correct methodology is more important than the conclusion, and I'm not at all suggesting that this is 100 percent the case. But that's not say there isn't a grain of truth in this statement, and it could go a long way towards helping the reader to understand how the German mind actually works, and more importantly *why* they make certain choices above others — choices that could appear baffling to an expat, but seem perfectly normal to a German person.

From a very early age, every good German child will

"Das darf man nicht"

have been taught the most fundamental phrase they will ever learn in their lifetime, one which will shape most of their adult life. In Germany, this fundamental question is — *am I allowed to do it?* I've lost count of the number of times I've seen a little child's innocent curiosity shot down in an instant and even reprimanded by his annoyed parent with the sentence, *"Das darf man nicht"* (It's not allowed.) I suppose, for a country built upon *rules and regulations,* nothing can be more important, so it's vital that its citizens understand the difference between *right* and *wrong.* Indeed, what could be more important for a functioning, thriving society? By teaching this basic principle to children from a very young age, society achieves its goal of making sure that nobody steps out of line. In Germany, things are generally very simple: they are either right or wrong, black or white. And so, decision-making becomes very easy, because your calculations are based on only two variables. Germany is not England or the US, where the answer depends on whom you speak to, who you know, and how much money you've got to spend. Rules are rules, they are absolute, and they apply to everyone. Isn't that what we all want from a truly democratic society?

In retrospect, I can think of several countries, Russia being one of them — incidentally, where I was born and lived for the first ten years of my life — where the reverse is true. Rules and regulations are made for the working and middle classes, but don't apply to the upper echelons of society, which also includes politicians. They can do as they please. This includes things like preferential treatment pretty much anywhere; not paying taxes; and even getting away with hit-and-runs, just because you have ties with the *top people*.

Naturally, nobody would want the *Russian* scenario playing out in their country, and I am not in any way suggesting that that would be a better option. There is, however, one downside to the rule-abiding mindset: people don't ask the *why* question. And Germany is probably the number one example of a country where people don't ask enough of these questions. Rules govern society, and questioning the rules for a *good* German is a complete *no-no*. Naturally, there are exceptions, and even in a law abiding country like Germany there are bound to be a select few who decide to rebel against the system. The G20 protests in Hamburg in 2017, and more recently the anti-coronavirus lockdown protests in Berlin, show us just that. But in the grand scheme of things, the German population can be used as a leading example for 'sticking to the rules'. The advantage to this from a governing point of view is that people will *do as they're told*. The downside — the overreliance on rules and regulations — in the best case scenario will cause absurdity where common sense does not prevail. In the worst case scenario — and we don't have to look too far back to dig out an example of that — cunning statesmen can take advantage by imposing a Rule of Law which benefits their goals, safe in the knowledge that people will abide by them without making too much fuss or asking too many questions.

Thou Shalt Report!

There are a few traits that could be exclusively attributed to the Germans as part of their inherent DNA: clarity, the constant need to explain everything, reliability, and, fourthly, reporting. This last point is one that I find particularly vexing, primarily because I was brought up with a mindset that is the polar opposite. Only last week, for instance, I opened up my school inbox — the one that still looks like it was stuck in the the nineties in terms of its design and interface — to discover that I had a new email from a certain Hubert Rinklaken, which was directed only to me, a fact which is in itself enough to get you a little nervous. Mr Rinklaken, as it turned out, was the class teacher of 8A, the class that I taught a music lesson to earlier that day. In his very cordial email, Mr Rinklaken explained to me that there had been reports of me not wearing a mask in the classroom, which had been a requirement for all students and teachers alike for a few weeks. Mr Rinklaken did not elaborate on the report, nor did he mention the specific instance to which this report referred. I therefore began frantically trying to think of a time when I had possibly moved my mask down a few centimetres to get some fresh air, even for a split millisecond. But eventually I managed to reassure myself that this definitely hadn't happened. And then the answer came to me: that very same day I had been giving out the half-term grades and, for some strange reason, around this time of year the number of complaints against teachers increases exponentially — matched only by the number received in June, for similar reasons, I should think.

This made me think about countless number of times I've witnessed kids 'snitching' on one another — most of the time they don't even bother doing it behind their backs, but are quite happy to do it in the *open*, and without any feeling of regret or fear of being *battered* by the other kids on their way home. On the contrary, I notice that this kind of behaviour is strongly encouraged by their teachers, parents, and everyone else around them. Telling on one's peers seems like a perfectly normal thing to do in Germany, especially if they have stepped out of line, or done something they shouldn't have. This behaviour is also evident in German adults, particularly if you think about the amount of people who call the *Ordnungsamt* as soon as they see their neighbours doing something they shouldn't, down to the most trivial things like not sorting their rubbish properly. If you encounter such behaviour, there is absolutely no point in getting upset at the person, calling them *Judas*, or questioning their friendship. You simply need to understand that this is a typical German behaviour trait, cultivated from an early age, and in the mind of the *Bundesrepublik*, there is absolutely nothing wrong with it. To understand this from a social point of view, it is perhaps better to think of it as a loyalty pyramid. Indeed, loyalty to the German state comes before loyalty to one's peers, and thus, anything that jeopardises the status quo will be treated according to those priorities.

Germans love dogs — fact! I have to admit, I hesitated for a second while writing this, as I was unsure as to

To summarise:

growing up in Germany as an adolescent inevitably involves three things: learning to follow the rules; mastering the art of self-reflection; and finally, understanding that no matter who it is, wrong means wrong, and you must report it to somebody with authority — as per the moral code of the Bundesrepublik.

Dogs & Germans

where in the book I should place this section. Some might say pets in general definitely belong to the 'leisure' sphere of one's life, and although that may be true for cats, hamsters, gerbils and perhaps even birds, I would definitely say that dogs are closer to being considered *family members* here in Germany. Indeed, Germany is a dog-crazy country, to the point of obsession — a true canine paradise. I can say this with absolute certainty, having observed dog owners here on many occasions. It would be safe to say that, in Germany, some dogs have better lives than many people in developing countries.

But don't take my word for it — take a look for yourselves. All you have to do is to go to a website that sells them, such as DeineTierwelt or eBay, and see the level of information that dog sellers request from potential buyers — your jaw will drop. For example, let's take the most popular breed in Germany, a pedigree black labrador. The advert states that a proud mother-labby is expected to give birth in a few months. Potential buyers need to send an email and include their personal information — as in, write who they are and what they do. In addition, they need to explain their current living situation, where they live, and how much space they have. They should also state why they think they would be a perfect fit for their new family member. Not to mention the fact that they would need to part with a few thousands euros to obtain the new-born. It might seem mad to you — it certainly does to me — but here in Germany people seem more than willing to oblige: they wouldn't even raise an eyebrow at these requirements. In fact, in recent years, the demand for dogs has gone through the roof. According to the website Statista, almost nine million households in Germany have a dog, and no fewer than 1.3 million have two dogs. Compare that to the 9.3 million households that do not have a four-legged friend.

It goes without saying that all dogs in Germany have their own passports; they are also microchipped and vaccinated shortly after birth. Furthermore, all dog owners must have pet insurance and pay dog tax for a bargain price of at least ninety euros per annum. Once you've become a proud dog owner, paid all your taxes and got all the documents, it's time to register your puppy with a dog trainer. Although this is not obligatory per se, you'd be well advised to do so — how else are you going to get your dog to follow all the German rules?

"Unleash your Dog!"

In most public places, dogs must be leashed, unless there are specific signs that tell you otherwise. There is an exception to the rule: you can get an actual written exemption for your dog called the '*Gehorsamsprüfung*' (obedience test) if you have proven that your dog is well-behaved and does not pose any danger to other members of the public. That's an actual thing! And from what I've seen here in Germany, dogs are model citizens, following the rules better than some humans. I'll never forget the time I crossed the road on red and, out of the corner of my eye, saw an older gentleman with his dog on the other side of the street. Both were waiting patiently for the green light and — you might think I've gone *barking mad,* if you'll excuse the pun — I swear the dog was giving me a dirty look, exactly the same look of shame and disbelief that I was getting from her owner. They were probably thinking that I should be on a leash myself.

If you see a dog being walked outside, you'll inevitably witness their owners following obediently behind, picking up their poop. Although such a spectacle is completely normal in the *Bundesrepublik,* and indeed in many other countries, it does make me wonder – "who really is at the top of the food chain?"

For a long time, I've been asking myself the big question — why Germany? Why do people all over the world want to come and live in this country? What makes

Chapter 7
Why Germany

it so special, particularly for non-German speakers? Is it the thriving job market, the generous social system, or perhaps the prospects of a comfortable life, free education and strong democratic values? Perhaps it is the family-oriented state sponsorship, or even the limitless autobahn? And more importantly: are these people merely tolerating their everyday cohabitation with the Germans, rationalising their feelings of *not fitting in*, and secretly wishing they would get a job offer elsewhere, back in their own country perhaps? Or are they genuinely happy with their lives in Germany and feel well integrated into their society and customs in the *Bundesrepublik?* I was adamant to find an answer to this question.

Having met my fair share of expats here in Germany, I tend to ask them quite directly — mostly out of sheer curiosity — what is it that they like about living in this country. Depending on who I ask, I get different responses — obviously — ranging from really enthusiastic and positive, through to those who are generally 'okay with everything'. A small share of interviewees claim they interact only with a tight-knit expat circle, working in jobs filled by expats, their contact with the real Germany limited to saying *"Hallo", "Danke"* and *"Tschüss"* to the cashier at the supermarket. The most common answers I got (when alcohol was not involved) were usually along the lines of "It's alright", or "Could be worse", or "Yeah, mate, can't complain". It's not a negative response, but it's not a convincing one either. I often sense an air of hesitation (i.e. they don't want to seem ungrateful), followed by a sense of resignation; like a climber who has reached base camp at Mount Everest, only to realise they don't have enough provisions for the whole journey, and so they have to turn back. Analogy aside, after a few pints, the floodgates tend to open and the comments begin to strike closer to the real sentiment: something along the lines of "bloody Germans" or "if you can't beat them, join them." The best one I've heard to date: "Germany would be the best country in the world, if there weren't quite as many Germans living here." During one such venture to the *Fleetenkieker* — an Irish pub, as you might have guessed — I asked Patrick, an Irish friend, about the things he misses most about Ireland. He said that the Irish are a bit more easy-going, not so serious and strict about rules, and can just 'have a laugh' now and then. Incidentally, Patrick is married to a German woman and they live happily together with their two wonderful children, or at least that is the image they project to the outside world. On the other hand, when I asked a Russian friend about Germany, she mentioned different things altogether. She said that she was very happy in Germany: "Everything is clear and structured; the system works." It sounded to me as though she was doing a direct comparison to her own country — mother-Russia, where it's not all *hunky-dorey,* imagine that! And finally, an Egyptian friend always comes up with the same answer when posed this question: "It's cold, and it rains a lot!" Indeed, living in the northern part of Germany does involve having to cope with the rain on any given day of any given month. But that's just the way it is, you can't change the weather, can you? At least not yet.

Looking at another source of information — namely Facebook expat groups — it's quite common to see people praise the practical side of living in Germany, but it's much harder to find positive posts based on *emotions*, like, "Oh I'm so happy in Germany, the people are really great, warm and friendly, and I really feel like I'm one of them". All the praise is mostly based on logic and reason, rarely on emotions. Granted, it's not that common to post emotional outbursts on Facebook — at least, not about your adoptive country; rejoicing and dancing around the proverbial tree, singing the German government's praises and gushing about how wonderful everything is, and how privileged expats should feel for being allowed to live in this wonderful country. But even so, there appears to be a pattern when it comes to expats in Germany.

It's easy to jump the gun here based on your initial experience with the Germans, i.e. the encounters you've had in supermarkets, at traffic lights, at work, or in any other public setting. It would be much harder to see beyond that initial *first impression;* beyond all the logic and pragmatism; beyond all the rules and 'das darf man nicht'. But if you can overcome the initial urge to dismiss the whole nation at the first opportunity as 'rude recycling-obsessed bio-food droids', you'll discover quite a different side to them, full of humour, emotion and joy. The important thing here is to have a real go at it.

It goes without saying that German language plays a vital role in your ability to integrate and make German friends — like it would in any other country. As we learned in Chapter 3, getting to grips with German is not easy by any means. In fact we can safely say that it is *bloody difficult.* If the prospect of learning the grammar and the prepositions doesn't put you off, then the countless compound nouns, the pronunciation and the tone definitely will. As a complete novice, things might seem easy at first, mainly due to the fact that the moment you say something in German, people recognise that you're a foreigner and immediately switch to English. Paradoxically, once you get past a certain level of German proficiency, you'll suddenly notice that your grace period is over and you're expected to know pretty much everything that gets thrown at you (see the chapters on the *Baumarkt* and *government offices*). That's when things start to get tricky. And yet, it is safe to say that language is key to understanding Germany's culture and its citizens, and certainly a good way of feeling more *au fait* with your new environment.

Setting the emotional aspects and the language aside — and perhaps the humour as well — let's take a look at Germany with the sombre eye of the *pragmatist,* and see what makes this country so *German* – which, to me, means a bastion of peaceful and modern democratic values, with a thriving economy, a high degree of social responsibility and a forward–looking society. Oh, and did I mention the free press?

German Media — DER SPIEGEL

Having recently watched the circus-like debate between the former President Donald Trump and the then presidential candidate Joe Biden, in which neither candidate managed to complete a full sentence without being interrupted by the other (although in Trump's case, a sentence never exceeded five words, which he repeated without conjugation or any proper sentence structure), I quietly sat on my sofa scrolling through the SPIEGEL app on my phone. In the era of Twitter, TikTok, YouTube and Facebook, where anyone can say pretty much anything and find people who agree with them; where hashtags, tags and provocative pictures are far more important than actual substance; and where many media outlets appear to have given up the fight, succumbing to the role of sensationalists bloggers, SPIEGEL — akin to John Wayne in one of the old Westerns — navigates its course through treacherous terrain, its dogged and unrelenting character a stark reminder to the lawless hoodlums, thieves and murderers that this is not their town. Whether or not you like my metaphor, everyone who has read an article published by the German media outlet DER SPIEGEL will agree that to this day they have produced (and keep on producing) some of the best journalism on this planet: always impartial and informative, and never misleading (well apart from that one journalist Claas Relotius, who faked most of his stuff. I'm going to use the 'a few bad apples' metaphor and hope the reader will accept this as a legit reason). With incredible attention to detail, their dogged investigative journalists have gained a reputation for uncovering some of the worst scandals in modern-day history, including the FIFA scandal, the Panama Papers and the Deutsche Bank scandal, to name a few.

To every German, SPIEGEL is unanimous with the *truth*. It symbolises what Germany has become in the last seventy years or so — a democracy where freedom of expression is valued above anything else. On a par with an independent judiciary system, free press forms a cornerstone of upholding democratic values, and there isn't a better example of this than SPIEGEL. Nobody would ever question the impartiality or the legitimacy of its journalism. There are no political parties that would dismiss it as being too leftist, and equally it wouldn't be criticised by liberals for being affiliated with the conservatives in any shape or form.

Although far from being a scholarly publication, as far as the length and difficulty is concerned, DER SPIEGEL has always maintained a high standard of language, requiring at least a C1 level of German language proficiency. This can be quite challenging, particularly to foreigners. Luckily, there is an English version of the app, which does translate some of the articles, though the choice is, understandably, limited. One thing is certain; you won't see any tabloid headings that jump out at you, nor will you see any intriguing photos that would otherwise fulfil the *clickbait* function. Instead, you will see paragraphs of text — very old school, I know — which you actually have to read yourself, think about the content, draw your own conclusions, and make up your own mind on the subject matter.

Reasonable, practical & a bit boring

German people are often described as reasonable, practical and — a bit boring. Constantly fine-tuning their processes, Germany is all about practicalities and reason. This trait is ingrained into every part of their everyday lives: whether at home, at work, at the home depot, or in a public place; whether this concerns their personal or public appearance or relationships, stretching from north to south, and even when they are abroad on holiday. Although the Germans themselves might not agree with you, by and large this is how they are perceived by foreigners. Every action has a logical reasoning behind it, and it has been thoroughly calculated, diagnosed and evaluated. You can always reason with a German person, and even if they disagree with you, they will always listen and respect you for having an opinion. There is a well-known German saying that puts this in a nutshell: "Although I completely disagree with what you are saying, I will fight for your right to be able to speak". This, after all, is a real democracy, and that is how a democracy works.

If you ever drop your wallet, or some other personal item in the street, pray that it gets picked up by a German person, because if that happens, they'll most certainly take it to a police station and hand it in. Even if it's out of their way and they don't really have the time, they'll still do it, on account of their strong moral compass. There is even a very high probability of you getting back all of the cash in your wallet as well.

It is a known fact that Germany is among the least corrupt nations in the world. I've spent a lot of the time contemplating the German system and comparing it to other European and non-European countries. Granted, socio-economic factors play a part in this, but that on its own would not be enough. You would still need to instill a very high degree of social responsibility, not to mention morality, into the population before it gets into their sub-consciousness and is triggered automatically. Indeed, the Germans have been working on this for quite some time. As we've seen, the educational system plays a great part as well. From a very early age, German children are taught responsibility, tolerance and *rules*. In particular they are taught things in a straight-forward manner — things are either *wrong* or *right*. There is no inbetween, no grey areas and nothing left to the imagination. And if they don't re-spect the rules, there will be somebody who will be com-pelled to remind them of them, with consequences always attached as a form of punishment, hence the compulsion to *tell people off.*

Germans place a high priority on structure, privacy and punctuality. The German people embrace the values of thriftiness, hard work and industriousness and there is great emphasis on making sure that "the trains run on time." According to Passport to Trade 2.0, an online business etiquette guide by the University of Salford in Manchester, England,   "Germans are most comfortable when they can organize and compartmentalize their world into controllable units. Time, therefore, is managed carefully, and calendars, schedules and agendas must be respected." I've illustrated how easy it is to throw the Germans off by doing something even slightly out of hand, for instance not following the process to the letter, or arriving a few minutes late.

Germans are stoic people who strive for perfectionism and precision in all aspects of their lives, even when it comes to their personal relationships They do not admit faults, even jokingly, and rarely hand out compliments. At first their attitude may seem unfriendly, even arrogant perhaps, but once you've got over your initial reaction and learnt to accept it, you'll notice that they are warm and friendly, always ready to help, and with a good — albeit very different — sense of humour. Germans have a strong sense of community, a social conscience and a desire to belong. To illustrate these points, the next chapter looks at some socio-economic and anthropological studies, which compare Germany and its people with other nations.

The Big Survey

In a recent survey published by the American media outlet *U.S. News,* which compared different countries in sixty-five different categories, Germany came in at number four overall. That's pretty impressive. The ranking was assembled by giving each attribute a score between 0 and 100, and then adding them up. A total of 20,000 people across the globe took part in the survey, and gave Germany an average score of 96.5 out of 100. The sixty-five attributes were grouped into nine categories that determined a country's overall ranking: Adventure, Citizenship, Cultural Influence, Entrepreneurship, Heritage, Movers (predicting a country's future growth), Open for Business, Power and Quality of Life.

It wasn't surprising at all to discover that Germany scored highly on all aspects of business, entrepreneurship, and power. With an annual GDP of $4 trillion, Germany is certainly the biggest economic power in Europe, and behind only the US, the UK and Russia on the world stage. Germany also scored highly in other categories such as education and quality of life, which took into account factors like access to food and housing, quality of education, healthcare, sustainable employment, job security, political stability, individual freedoms and environmental quality.

On the flipside — although Germany boasts a highly skilled, affluent workforce, the country's population is aging, raising many questions about the increasing cost of social welfare, and the high financial burden on future generations. Equally unsurprising was the fact that Germany scored very badly in the adventure category, coming in a meagre 50th place in the world rankings. This category measured the country's *Wanderlust* (ironic considering the borrowed word comes from the German language) — this is, their desire to be adventurous, travel, explore, and generally get away from daily routines. It also ranked the destination according to attributes such as *friendly, fun, pleasant climate, scenic and sexy*. I'm guessing not everyone has managed to look beyond the lack of pleasantries and the stern and serious façade of the Germans like I have. *Being adventurous* could also be interpreted as being more spontaneous, less predictable, and taking more risks. As you can imagine, those three things are very un-German-like, hence why they scored so badly on this. Luckily for the citizens of the *Bundesrepublik*, however, the *Adventure* category only amounted to 2 percent of the total points.

Germany ranked in the top ten for citizenship. This category considered parameters such as human rights, gender equality, religious freedoms, and a trustworthy and well-distributed political power. High-scoring countries are therefore exemplary in upholding values that are worth imitating, inspiring pride in their citizens, civil society leaders and lawmakers alike. Another word for this is *civilised*. A civilised society epitomises and embodies these qualities, while an *uncivilised* one reflects the opposite, e.g. dictatorship, lawlessness, censorship, racism, and so forth. If I refer you back to the section on how German children are educated, then this notion makes perfect sense. Accepting other people's opinions, not interrupting, respecting each other, raising awareness of multiculturalism and religious freedoms — all of this forms the backbone of how Germans want their democratic society to function, and it works. It might have a few side effects such as having to patiently listen to their mind-bogglingly tedious monologues forever on end, but this is still the better option than the one we were recently presented with in the *Trump* vs. *Biden TV* debate, wouldn't you agree?

The Citizenship category also looked at personal responsibility, trustworthiness and caring about the environment. As an eye-witness, I can certainly attest to this. As documented throughout this book, there are few nations that possess such a high grade of moral and social responsibility as the Germans do, although they sometimes tend to take it a bit too far for my liking. Telling others off for doing something they shouldn't is part of that too. In Germany, there is no excuse for disobeying the *red man,* throwing plastic rubbish into the paper container, or even stating things that are not entirely correct. In contrast to other countries where people would *think twice* before *being rude* to a complete stranger, the law-abiding citizens of the federal republic won't hesitate to quickly point out — in private or in public — that your words or actions are not in line with the norm. Better think again before you decide to go against the grain.

Hofstede insights

Another way of looking at Germany is through the lens of Hofstede's cultural dimensions theory, which is a framework for cross-cultural communication. Essentially, it shows the effects of a society's culture on the values of its members, and how these values relate to behaviour, using a structure derived from factor analysis. To elaborate, Geert Hofstede worked for one of the biggest tech companies of his time — IBM. While working there in the eighties, he conducted one of the largest-ever multilingual surveys (this was long before Facebook, Twitter, and even the internet itself). He collated data under six different headings, and then used them to compare nations, depending on which end of the scale they were closest to. The six categories were: Power Distance, Individualism, Masculinity, Uncertainty Avoidance, Long Term Orientation, and Indulgence. Figure 1, below, shows how Germany is portrayed in relation to these factors.

Fig. 4 Cultural Dimensions

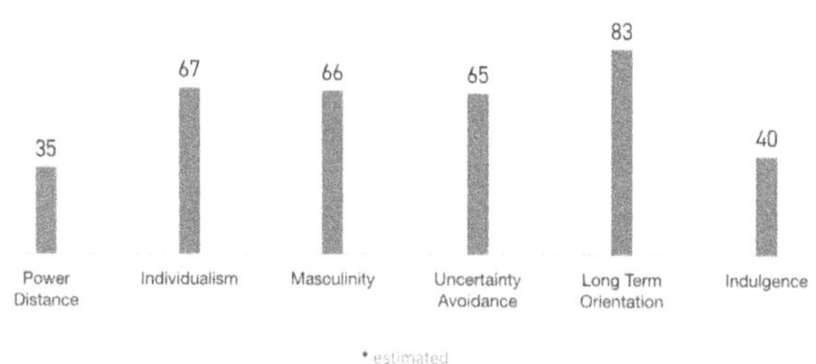

Source: Germany https://www.hofstede-insights.com

So what can we say about Germany based on this graph?

Essentially, it aims to answer some fundamental questions with regard to its society and how it operates. What drives the Germans on an individual and a group level? Is power distributed equally? What defines the value system upon which the society is measured? And how do its people deal with the uncertainty factors? Let's examine each point individually.

Power Distance

The extent to which the less powerful members of institutions and organisations within a country expect and accept that power is distributed unequally.

Evidently, Germany achieves a low score on this. On the one hand, this is evidence of its democratic, dialogue-focused and method-based approach. On the other, it shows a less centralised management style, in which everyone can voice their opinion directly to the top. Flat hierarchies are preferred to outdated and overcomplicated systems; although, as we have seen throughout this book, this does not always apply to large and traditional multi-nationals, as well as government institutions. On a social level, people will not hold back to tell you exactly what they think, which can be good or bad, depending on your own experience and upbringing. The main consensus, however, is that everyone enjoys equal freedoms, which, after all, is the pretext of a modern, democratic society. This makes Germany an attractive destination to foreigners, particularly those who come from countries whose governments are less open to such entrepreneurial spirit, seeking to control everything. One downside to this approach could be the lack of accountability, particularly in customer-client relations, of which we have seen several examples in this book. In hindsight, getting crap service at a restaurant, or not getting your way with customer services, is a small price to pay for all of the perks, wouldn't you agree?

Individualism

The degree of interdependence a society maintains among its members.

According to Hofstede, German society is a truly individualist one and scored a high sixty-seven out of one hundred on this. There is a strong belief in the ideal of self-actualisation, i.e. reaching your maximum potential as an individual, on an intellectual as well as a materialistic level. Loyalty is based on personal preferences for people as well as a sense of duty and responsibility. We have seen evidence of this sense of duty transcending far beyond people's working lives, and into their social environment. Hence why Germans are so compelled to tell complete strangers off if they are doing something they aren't supposed to — like crossing at the red light, or throwing a plastic bottle into the wrong container. This ties in nicely with the notion that Germans are the most direct in the world, following the ideal to be "honest, even if it hurts" — and thus giving people a fair chance to learn from their mistakes. This particular behaviour trait often antagonises expats, who are not used to being told 'what not to do'. However, on a societal level, this creates a safety blanket; one where you can rest assured that things will get done properly, and your lost wallet will find its way back to you. Just don't get upset next time a German person gives you advice, even if you never asked for it.

Masculinity

A high score on this dimension indicates that a society will be driven by competition, achievement and success, with success being defined by the winner / best in field — a value system that starts in school and continues throughout organisational life.

With a score of 66, Germany is considered a masculine society. This emphasis upon performance is nurtured from childhood — as early as the age of ten, when children are streamed into different school systems. People 'live in order to work' and draw a lot of self-esteem from their tasks. Managers are expected to be decisive and assertive. Status is often shown, especially by cars, watches and technical devices. Although this is not the case for many smaller companies and those who have tried to reinvent themselves to fall in with modern times, you'll notice this trend in more traditional firms; those genuinely reluctant to change. You need to look no further than large telecommunication companies, insurance companies, banks, the car industry, and pretty much all of the civil service. There is the stereotype of a 50-something male boss; tall, broad-shouldered, very formal and — to be a bit cheeky — with a schtick up his arse. But I shouldn't be overly negative. After all, the masculinity factor stimulates an environment of achievers, and a lot of Germany's economic success wouldn't have been possible if it weren't for precisely those stereotypical figures. These factors make Germany a highly desirable destination for skilled workers from abroad: engineers, app developers, architects, programmers, economists, and even musicians (sorry, I couldn't help myself).

Uncertainty Avoidance

The dimension Uncertainty Avoidance has to do with the way that a society deals with the fact that the future can never be known: should we try to control the future or just let it happen?

Definitely my favorite dimension when talking about Germany. As I've illustrated, Germans despise the unknown. It starts from the very core — their language: the way the words have an exact meaning to dispel any ambiguity; the way sentences are structured and the way they always explain everything in detail. This, combined with the Germans' inexorable obsession with planning and optimising and their preoccupation with their health and insurance, are all indicative of a nation that strives to always be in control. This might also explain why the Germans are so afraid of admitting mistakes. If you want to test this — just for a laugh — next time you're waiting for a big meeting, ask your German colleague in passing about some made-up topic not on the agenda, and then watch them get really nervous. In all likelihood, they will panic a bit, start going through their emails on their phone, looking for non-existent clues of a thing you just made up, and then barrage you with questions. To foreigners, for reasons mentioned above, Germans may appear a bit control-freak-y, and this might become a problem, particularly for those who are not used to having the next two years of their lives meticulously planned and documented in a calendar; or those who are more used to a 'let's just see what happens' approach. This might not only affect their professional environment, but also their personal relationships, as seen in the previous chapter.

Long Term Orientation

Germany's high score of eighty-three indicates that it is a pragmatic country. In societies with a pragmatic orientation, people believe that truth depends very much on situation, context and time. They show an ability to adapt traditions easily to changed conditions, a strong propensity to save and invest, thriftiness, and perseverance in achieving results.'

Just consider the fact that by the 1950s, Germany was on its knees economically. After losing two world wars it was ruined and humiliated as a nation. And yet, several generations later, the country has established itself not only as a leading European economic power, but, more importantly, as a leading democratic nation. Germany's response to COVID-19 pandemic, which I experienced first-hand, is a masterclass of how a nation *should* act in such times of crisis, and can only be admired by others aspiring to be like them. "When the Germans have a problem, they make a plan".

Indulgence

The extent to which people try to control their desires and impulses.

From a very young age, German children are taught important values like respect, obedience, restraint, cultural diversity, and of course the all-important *"NEIN, das darf man nicht!"* phrase. Germany's low score in this category indicates that German culture is restrained in nature, and reaffirms its strong control over desires and impulses. The upshot of this is that Germans are grateful for pretty much anything, and you will never be judged for bringing a cheap bottle of 'vino nobile' as a house-warming gift. There is a downside, however, and we've seen this in many aspects of everyday life in the *Bundesrepublik*: from the bulky-looking pastries at the bakery that lack that 'va-va-voom' appeal, through to the notion that customers are definitely *not* kings, and are *always wrong*. As a foreigner, you'll be expected to fall in line with this view, so prepare to be scrutinised by an army of *Mr Schmidt agents* – to use The Matrix analogy.

Chapter 8
Conclusion –
the adaptation cycle

One of the things I have gradually come to realise is that, when living in a foreign country, a person goes through a so-called adaptation cycle. This cycle begins with an obvious resistance to all things new, until it reaches a state of partial or full acceptance, and finally, it turns the 'new' into the norm. This applies to every part of your surrounding environment, and foods are no exception. And so, whether it is the ominous *Currywurst*, or curry-flavoured ketchup, banana-flavoured beer, or any other food that seems weird at first, eventually you learn to accept them, and even start enjoying them, if only just a little.

The important variable in this equation is age. There is a reason why young people are far more able to adapt to new environments, languages and cultures than those who are in their thirties and upwards. Most likely, this is the reason that older people are often accused of *being set in their* ways, and lashing out at everything that threatens to change their status quo. You don't have to be a rocket scientist to figure out exactly why that is, so I'm going to spare you the details.

And so, if you want to truly *embrace* another culture, your best chance is to do it while you still fall into one of these age brackets: adolescent, teenager, or young adult. The same reasoning is used in the argument that children up to the age of eleven, when immersed into a new environment — provided they get enough exposure to the target language — are able to become *native speakers*. I can attest to this, being one such specimen. When I was ten years old, my family moved to Sweden, and I was fully immersed into life in the countryside: the Swedish language, dancing round the midsummer tree, a strange sport called floorball and a funny way of saying yes while breathing in. The point is, if you plan to settle in Germany with children, do not send them to international schools with other foreign children. Instead, give them the chance to integrate, learn the language and the values, and experience local culture first-hand. They will thank you for it later.

For much of this book I poked fun at the Germans from an *I-am-British-and-why-can't-you-take-a-joke* stance. And a lot of things do add up when you look at them individually. Humour in Germany will never be at the same level as it is in Britain, the US, Australia, or any other Anglo-Saxon region. It will never become an essential part of daily life, ingrained into every aspect of your communication with others — be it at work, in public, or within your own four walls. Yet, over the years, as I have become more interested in politics, history and general *dad stuff* like *The History Channel, National Geographic,* and reading 'the news', I've increasingly become an admirer of Germany and its citizens, on both an individual level and a national scale.

I have come to believe that there is no other nation in the world that cultivates such a high moral compass in its inhabitants from a very early age, and continuously throughout their adult lives, teaching them good traits that have almost become alien elsewhere, like the notion of *respect towards peers and adults;* tolerance, patience, diversity and cultural awareness; religious freedom; and climate awareness, to name a few. Indeed, as a foreigner you might be shocked initially when a complete stranger berates you openly on the street for crossing the red man, or throwing a piece of rubbish on the floor, or even honking their horn at you for not concentrating at the traffic lights. But, to Germans, as I've already mentioned, this constitutes part of their moral obligation to their community, city and state. It is their exemplary conduct in this respect that sets them apart from almost every other nation in the world.

The clarity of their language is another one. The way it is constructed: clear, unambiguous, descriptive, leaves no room for misinterpretation. If it is written YOU MUST NOT DO THIS, then there is no vagueness, no misunderstanding, no 'read between the lines', and no '*yes but no but*'. The rules are the same for everyone, and everyone is expected to follow them in exactly the same manner, without exemption. At a time when the world has reached a new level of stupidity, with its leaders seemingly keen on sowing division, stoking hatred and inciting violence among its population, mostly resorting to foul, sensationalist language, the German Chancellor Angela Merkel leads by example. Her leadership style, demeanour and language (including body language), all encompass the values crucial to this country, which are cultivated in its citizens from early on in their educational process.

Granted, Germany is not a perfect country, not by any means. It has its flaws too, and if you intend to make this country your home in the near future — whichever part of the world you are from — you need to think long and hard if it is the right country for you. In the beginning Germany can seem like a joyless place: its citizens distinctly lacking a sense of humour, spontaneity, excitement and *joie de vivre* in general. However, if you can adapt to this part of life (even though it might not be an easy task to do), you can reap the great benefits this country has to offer, perhaps greater than anywhere else in the world. Whether it's job security, high living standards, excellent and free education, secure pensions, freedom of speech, equality or political stability — all of this has only been made possible due to the consistently unified, concerted, and disciplined efforts of its citizens — the way the whole system has been set up in this country for many decades.

According to Britannica, 'Much of Germany's post-World War II success has been the result of the renowned industriousness and self-sacrifice of its people, of which novelist Günter Grass, winner of the Nobel Prize for Literature in 1999, remarked, "To be a German is to make the impossible possible." He added, more critically:

For in our country everything is geared to growth. We're never satisfied. For us, enough is never enough. We always want more. If it's on paper, we convert it into reality. Even in our dreams we're productive.

This devotion to hard work has combined with a public demeanour — which is at once reserved and assertive — to produce a stereotype of the German people as aloof and distant. Yet Germans prize both their private friendships and their friendly relations with neighbours and visitors, place a high value on leisure and culture, and enjoy the benefits of life in a liberal democracy that has become ever more integrated with and central to a united Europe.

Ultimately, the decision on whether or not this country is suitable for you is a highly subjective one. Much that will depend on your own persona and the kind of experience you've had throughout your life prior to moving here. If you're a pragmatist, it's easy to see all the benefits of living in this country, as I'm sure you'll agree. On the other hand, practical reasons on their own are not enough to make us feel happy in our new habitat. Being human beings as we all are, we also need to feel like we truly belong here, and for that we would need to really integrate into the environment surrounding us. Connecting with the local people is an important step toward that integration, and for that one would have to go much further than merely saying *"Hallo"* and *"Tschüss"* to the cashier at your local supermarket. I would suggest taking in as much of the surroundings as you possibly can: be a tourist in your own city, at least for the first year. Explore its nature, food, culture and language and be open-minded about it. Granted, there are certain things that you might never fully get used to, like the honking cars, scolding strangers, customer services, crippling bureaucracy, or even the fact that you have to sit down to pee. But in all fairness, these are the elements you can't change, so instead of fuming about it, you can change the degree to which you react to it. Accepting them for what they are will take you a long way in the right direction. It's easy to go on Facebook and vent your frustration on an expat group, and I'm sure, within minutes you'll find plenty of sympathisers who also feel the same way you do. It's much harder to try to understand the culture and the mindset of the Germans, and then... accept it for what it is. Throughout the course of this book, my aim has been precisely that, and I hope that the reader will find it a useful stepping stone in their effort to integrate into German society. After all, this country and its people have got so much to offer, and it would be a shame not to take advantage of that opportunity.

PS. and yet, if all fails, and you would rather make stupid inapropriate jokes about *Ze German*, along with Hitler salutes, then you can just take your stuff and b*gger off back to where you came from! Having just said that, I've just finished packing my last removal box. *Tschüss!*

How German are you?
The ultimate test

Here's something for expats living in Germany: how do you know when you've been in Germany too long? If you answer yes to eight or more questions, then it's time to buy yourself a pair of *Lederhosen* and change your surname to Schmidt.

- You enjoy curry-flavoured ketchup.
- You own a Jack Wolfskin jacket.
- You recycle your bottles, and separate the rubbish accordingly.
- When you answer the phone you say your last name first.

- You know where Chemnitz is on a map.
- You arrange a dinner with your friends several weeks in advance, and send everybody your address with a Google Maps printout.
- Your way of thinking has changed from results-oriented to process-oriented. In other words it is more important to follow a structure and do everything 'as instructed', rather than actually getting a result.
- You don't mind watching an English series in German.
- You've stopped apologising.
- You've got a *Haftpflichtversicherung*.
- You NEVER cross at a red light.
- You go to your doctor at least twelve times a year.
- You know what the words *Bescheinigung* and *Gutachten* mean.
- You always follow up with an explanation e.g. 'weil', or 'because'.
- You capitalise all nouns.
- You spell English words with 'sch' instead of 'sh'.
- You say *"Aua"* when you get hurt.
- And last but not least, you think that making Hitler jokes is inappropriate.

ABOUT AUTHOR

Fadi Gaziri is a musician, educator, composer, music producer, business owner and a linguist. He has spent the last 20 years living and creating in Germany.

International Background

Born to a Russian mother and a Lebanese father, Fadi spent his formative years in the Soviet Union before fleeing the country with his parents to Sweden. After absorbing the Scandinavian culture for 4 years he relocated to the UK. After graduating from Durham University and Bournemouth University he subsequently moved to Hamburg where he eventually settled with his wife Stephanie.

He commands 5 languages fluently of which 4 are spoken at a native level these being English, Russian, Swedish and German. Fadi has always been a great fan of satire. As a young adult he was a big fan of Bill Bryson and Rowan Atkinson. He later acquired a taste for self-mockery: a type of comedic expression that was developed in the early 70s in Britain and peaked with the emergence of The Office, Little Britain, Flight of the Concords, and films by the Cohen Brothers.

As a British national living in Germany, Fadi found it difficult to adapt to the German way of life at first. He constantly bemoaned their lack of a sense of humour, the overly-direct approach; the lack of tact, the non-existence of customer-service, the staggering bureaucracy and many other aspects of everyday life one faces in the Bundesrepublik. However, where many of us expats would have packed our stuff and left, Fadi decided to 'stick it out'. Tired of banging his head against a wall he quietly decided to write a book.

"It was an epiphany. All of a sudden if I was frustrated with something, instead of venting it at other people, I wrote it down on a piece of paper - it was like meditating".

It turned out that Fadi was very frustrated indeed.

His style pays homage to Bill Bryson; written with a light anecdotal tone, often mixed in with a dollop of self-mockery, giving a vivid account of German society as a whole.